The Words
of Jesus

The Words of Jesus

A Gospel of the Sayings of Our Lord

With Reflections by
Phyllis Tickle

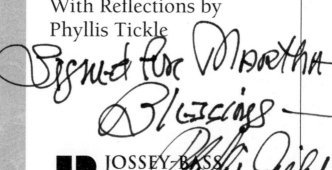

JB JOSSEY-BASS
A Wiley Imprint
www.josseybass.com

Published by Jossey-Bass
A Wiley Imprint
989 Market Street, San Francisco, CA 94103-1741—www.josseybass.com

Jossey-Bass books and products are available through most bookstores. To con-tact Jossey-Bass directly call our Customer Care Department within the U.S. at 800-956-7739, outside the U.S. at 317-572-3986, or fax 317-572-4002.

Jossey-Bass also publishes its books in a variety of electronic formats. Some con-tent that appears in print may not be available in electronic books.

Library of Congress Cataloging-in-Publication Data:

Tickle, Phyllis.
    The words of Jesus : a gospel of the sayings of Our Lord with reflections / by Phyllis Tickle.—1st ed.
        p. cm.
    Includes index.
    ISBN-13: 978-0-7879-8742-8 (cloth)
    1. Jesus Christ—Words. I. Title.
    BT306.T53 2008
    232.9'54—dc22

                                            2007044098

Printed in the United States of America
FIRST EDITION
HB Printing   10 9 8 7 6 5 4 3 2 1

CONTENTS

Jesus said, "I have said these things to you so that my joy may be in you, and that your joy may be complete."

—John 15:11 [II.50]

The Words
of Jesus

Reflections on the Words of Jesus

When I began this project almost two years ago, I was innocent about what it would cost me. That cost has not been, as one might expect, in study time and mental effort. Actually, I enjoyed the months of concentrated work. The cost has instead been in the nights I lay sleepless and wrestling, like Jacob, with new perceptions about what it is to be both Christian and a self at the same time. Initially the wrestling was more benign than that, of course. Initially it was, more than anything else, a kind of introspective curiosity about just why in the world I had taken on such a piece of work in the first place.

Compiling the "words" of Jesus—the red-letter portions of the four New Testament Gospels and the first chapter of the Acts of the Apostles—into a cohesive whole was not my idea originally, but it most certainly was one that from the start I embraced with enthusiasm. Now, all these months later, however, I suspect that my enthusiasm was more a reaction to latent frustrations than an eager engagement of the idea itself.

I am what is called nowadays a professional religionist. That is, I make my living studying and writing *about* religion, unlike theologians and pastors, who are pleased to say that they *do* religion. That is not an inconsequential distinction. The irony is that the men and women in either category almost always feel some kind of yearning to cross over into and poach on the other's territory. The problem is that neither cohort is equipped with the training and skills required to do the other's job. That shortcoming does not prevent the yearning or satisfy the itch to cross boundary lines, which is what apparently happened two years ago and has led to this compilation of Our Lord's words.

A colleague (another religionist) and I were having a midmorning break together during a professional meeting when she said to me, "Did you ever wonder what you would really find if you took out the duplications and triplications and connective tissue of the Gospels and stripped it all down again to just His words?" Even as I retype that question here, the sheer clarity of it opens something like a cavern in my heart and my soul. I am stunned all over again, even as I was that day.

No, I had never wondered such a thing. It would never have occurred to me that such a thing could even be done. I knew, as do most Western Christians, that the first gospels, both those that are now received as canonical and those that are not, began as "Sayings" gospels. That is, the earliest records of Jesus' words were just that—recordings of what He said. The ordering of when He said what and to whom as well as why and where were all added later as first the disciples and then the apostles began to fashion an accompanying biography that would make the words more easily and accurately remembered and assimilated—perhaps even make them more palatable. I did not suspect this last reason, however, until long after the pivotal conversation that first set me off on the unthinkable business of stripping away the biographies and returning to the Sayings alone.

Anyone who has ever picked up one of the noncanonical gospels such as, for example, the widely popular *Gospel of Thomas* or the hypothetical "Q" *Gospel* knows firsthand the power of the rat-a-tat-tat, pow-pow-pow presentation of a Sayings gospel. Devoid of narrative context, the Sayings come straight at us like so many bullets, piercing all our armor and destroying all our carefully thought-out prior convictions. There are at least some two dozen plus gospels now known to us, though most of them are less popularly circulated than is *Thomas* or "*Q.*" For various reasons that are tangential here, those gospels, whether Sayings or narratives, were either never admitted to the canon of Christian Scripture or were prayerfully drummed out of it over the early decades of the Church.[1] Being outside the canon now does not, however, diminish their outré appeal and, in the case of the Sayings gospels, their forcefulness.

As a devout and observant, if less than exemplary, Christian who is also a paid observer of religion, I have over the last few years had to read the noncanonical gospels that have been commercially published for the general market. I have felt compelled as well to read some of those that have not been so widely touted or advertised. I did not particularly like the process. Assessing sacred words primarily for their potential impact on popular theology and the commercial book market is sometimes distasteful at best. It is especially so when the words being assessed are those of one's own tradition. Even so, it didn't take much angst or much insight for me to understand the appeal and sheer naked power of what I was reading. I now think that that power was a bit like a

---

[1] One of the anticipated pleasures of compiling *The Words of Jesus* has been the possibility for engaging readers off the page as well as on it. If you are curious about side issues such as this one, please go to http://www.allthewordsofjesus.com, where you will find additional material on such topics as canonical establishment as well as the opportunity to blog about *The Words of Jesus* with other readers.

coiled snake that, staring at its victim, dares him or her to move, and in the moving, to be struck. Certainly *I* was struck, anyway. My original "What if?" became no longer a speculation but an irrepressible torment.

Like most writers and wordsmiths, I like intellectual puzzles that are word-based ones as opposed to those that are shape or number based. There is no question in my mind that this too was part of the early appeal here. It would be more self-congratulatory to say I was attracted to this work because of some deeply religious conviction, but that is, and was, just simply not true. Yes, I was annoyed—and consciously so—by the facile and almost unexamined public acceptance of the noncanonical gospels. But I was also fascinated by the potency of the Sayings format and drawn to the intellectual game and pleasure of trying to tease out just how and why that format works so well. May God have mercy on fools like me.

Dozens, perhaps even hundreds, of scholars—theologians and pastors, not religionists, in other words—have struggled over the centuries to create parallels among the canonical Gospels. That is, they have tried to integrate all the stories of Matthew, Mark, Luke, and John into a consistent and noncontradictory whole. That cannot be done. The Gospelers' stories will not line up either on a consistent timeline or on some kind of wall-chart outline of systematic theology. Whatever Jesus of Nazareth was and is, He is not, and never has been, a systematic theologian. At least He has not been in ways that can be engaged from inside the limitations of our human logic and vocabularies. This does not mean that Matthew, Mark, Luke, and John were inaccurate in what they recorded so much as it means that we are inaccurate, if not arrogant and stupid, in thinking that consistency is necessary, let alone a necessary restriction upon God. More probably, it now seems to me, consistency is a consolation slavishly desired by those of us who are still caught within time and the confines of personal perception. Ralph Waldo Emerson, who is not usually cited for his humor, famously made much the same point almost two hundred years ago by observing that, "a foolish consistency is the hobgoblin of little minds."

The fact that the work of scholars in trying to compose so-called "Gospel parallels" has always ended in a less than satisfactory manner did not stop me from using their work to further my own. Mine, however, was a different task. I set out not to correlate the details of each Gospeler's rendition of when and where Jesus said a thing with the details of the other Gospelers'. Rather, I set out to strip away all those renditions and variances in the reported circumstances and expose instead the words themselves. Of course that purpose has similar obstacles.

Even a child of ten or twelve studying for confirmation into the Christian family knows that what Jesus is reported as saying—that is, what the red-letter words report—is not always precisely the same thing or the same wording in two different Gospels. More often than not there is variation even when the Sayings being quoted in each Gospel quite obviously have a common root. Perhaps because the Beatitudes are the most widely known of Jesus' Sayings, the variations in them are often those most tellingly cited as proofs positive of scriptural inconsistencies. There is no question that the Beatitudes as recorded in Matthew are reported by Luke in wording that is different in form, though hardly in message or intent. For example, whereas Matthew reports Jesus as saying, "Blessed are the poor in spirit, for theirs is the Kingdom of God," Luke reports the first Beatitude as, "Blessed are you poor, for yours is the Kingdom of God." Even the list of the Beatitudes is not the same in both Gospels. But then I thought, what if? What if the two were merged?

And therein lay the trick, the tormenting question, the initial excitement, and eventually, the stark power of it all. In the merged Beatitudes, Matthew's "Blessed are the poor in spirit, for theirs is the Kingdom of God" is followed by Luke's "But woe to you who are rich, for you have received your consolation," together creating a clarity that will not admit of much waffling or variety of interpretation [I.4].[2] But it was in the course of merging variant texts such as the Beatitudes that I first began to get a glimmer of my own motivation in taking on the work in the first place.

Because the Beatitudes are indeed the most famous Sayings of Jesus, they are the ones most commonly subjected to popular as well as clerical dissection. They also occur early on in His public teachings and therefore early on in the Gospel. The merging of them into a whole was, as a result, the first of many times when I was forced to acknowledge a previously suppressed emotion in myself. Doing the work forced me to remember how many hundreds of times—literally—I had listened to preachers or Sunday School teachers or credentialed commentators tear Luke from Matthew or Matthew from Luke and then

---

[2] Throughout, the references in brackets are to the five books of Sayings contained in this volume. The roman numeral refers to the book cited; the Arabic numeral corresponds to the number of the saying.

try to attach some great doctrinal significance to there being two renditions of His words and two locales for their delivery.

At first, that remembering evoked in me the same kind of low-grade irritation I had been only half aware of for many years. What I had not previously realized, though, was that the low-grade irritation had apparently escalated into a major and very personal complaint. That is, I am not at all sure that talking about variants in the wordings of a Saying adds much to the soul's formation. I am very sure it takes something away, even if that something is only a sense of immediacy, perhaps even of intimacy. Consider, for instance, what would happen were one lover to stop caressing the other's face in order to discuss racial heritage, environmental conditions, and individual genetic and circumstantial backgrounds as determinants of human facial structure. Such an example, while it may seem extreme, is nonetheless very close to being an apt analogy for what I mean to convey. An intimacy has been interrupted, and a consummation delayed.

If anybody at all understands the danger, both professional and personal, that attaches to making such a statement as that in public and in print, it is I. At the very least I will be accused of naivete and anti-intellectualism. Heavens, I could argue that case against myself with as much ease and wit as anybody else, religionist or theologian. Yes, it is naive. Yes, it is anti-intellectual. Yes, I mean it nonetheless, or I mean something very close to it. We have become lost in a wilderness of scholarship that forgot to bring faith and humility along for the trek.

I do not know, or even think I know, what the Sayings of Jesus "mean" in some kind of global sense. I do know, especially now, what I think they mean, what I think Phyllis Tickle is being taught and told and given in and through them. I have few qualms about discussing the effect I find those words having on and in me; but God forbid that I or anybody else should ever assert as doctrine or infallible interpretation the reflections that follow here.

Beyond wanting to speak some of my own truths, though, there is something else I hope for even more. I hope in due course to overhear something of what others who worship Him have perceived and received through engaging the Sayings. I certainly hope that many of those who revisit the words of Jesus in this format will likewise want to discover what other Christians think and have perceived. This hope comes not because I believe that any single one of us has any more of a handle on absolute truth than do the rest of us. Rather, it comes from knowing beyond all doubt that we Christians are a community on earth and in time. And in this era of rapid communication and vast, informal exchanges of information, what each of us receives, accepts, and rejects is filtered over and into the whole body of the community. The result—the Church that emerges and is emerging—is, to borrow contemporary terms, an ongoing, open-source, self-organizing network or system. That system may be naive by traditional standards, but it is also alive, flexible, changing, growing, diverse, and egalitarian, all largely because it can never assume itself to be either finished or error-free. Employed prayerfully, its very lack of hierarchy can produce, and is already producing, a kind of fertile chaos along whose edges change and vitality find a nurturing natural habitat. It goes without saying, of course, that it has always been the edges where Jesus and His words have likewise found theirs.

There is, I would also suggest, a kind of naivete in thinking that theoretical scholarship is untouchable simply because it is scholarship. Likewise, there is a kind of fearful anti-intellectualism involved in accepting what is argued in theory as if it had been argued in truth and absolute fact. We have no trouble remembering this when we jest about the great, serious arguments of centuries ago over just how many angels can dance on the head of a pin. Yet doubtless most of us would have been careful with our scorn had we ourselves been alive when the arguments were being delivered.

In a way, then, what I have come to accept is something that I suspect I had long ago realized and been too chary to admit even to myself: namely, that much exegesis and even Jesus scholarship is metanarrative and, as such, has too long blocked faith from entering the narrative itself. One of the most poignant quotations of the whole twentieth century, for me anyway, is Albert Einstein's now-famous statement that God does not play dice with the universe. Trained in classical Newtonian physics, even the great Einstein could never set aside Enlightenment science's metanarratives of deterministic cause-and-effect or reductionism. As a result, he was forever blocked from taking, with men like Niels Bohr, Werner Heisenberg, and Max Born, the leap of faith that led to the discovery of quantum physics and its entirely different set of rules. The trick, it would seem, is and always has been to discern the difference between narrative and metanarrative; and that is not a task for the timid of heart or mind.

Which brings me to the next moment of truth that befell me early on in the work of compilation and merging texts: (What, then, are we to make of their blatant contradictions, for the contradictions are there?) For example, consider the woman who washed Jesus' feet with her tears, anointed them with precious perfume from an alabaster jar, then dried them with her hair. Was she a prostitute? Luke seems to think so. Matthew and Mark, as well as Luke, say she did this thing in the home of Simon, who was either a leper or a Pharisee or—who knows, maybe both. Simon's house seems to have been in Jerusalem or in Bethany. John says Bethany, but then John also says that the woman was Mary, sister of the resurrected Lazarus, and that the washing occurred in Lazarus's house. Now these are mutually exclusive details. What is patent in all of them, however, is that the words spoken to some woman at some dinner party somewhere mattered enough to the early circle of followers to be included in all their stories, albeit with different emphases on what Jesus is reported as having said.

What matters here first—what *has* to matter first and foremost—is that those words as recorded and handed down to us were written down by those who either knew Jesus or knew those who knew Him or, in the most extreme case, knew those who had known those who knew Him. It also matters that those Sayings as recorded were accepted by the early, early Church as accurate recordings. One can argue that there may have been—indeed, probably was—infiltration of human perception and purposes into the recorded text. It is still undeniably, however, the text that was validated and embraced by those who were intimately and biographically involved in receiving it and who judged it to be consonant with what was said. And it is the "to be consonant with what was said" that is the informing phrase here.

What great man or woman has ever posthumously enjoyed the luxury of a consistent biography? None, so far as I know. Look, for example, at the many "Lives of Lincoln" available today. Abraham Lincoln was assassinated within the full adulthood of my paternal grandfather and only some two dozen years before my father's birth. Lincoln has not, in other words, been dead so long that I myself cannot call up from personal memory family tales about him. Yet even given such proximity and even given the fact that there is considerable agreement among us about what Mr. Lincoln stood for and intended, there is not always unanimity of opinion about to whom and under what circumstances he said what. Just a casual look at some of those "Lives" will confirm that point.

Of as much, if not more, importance, however, is the fact that, sans video and audio recorders, there is no unimpeachable record of the intonation, inflection, and body language with which President Lincoln said what he said. Yet body language, inflection, and emotional intensity of delivery are part and parcel of meaning when we deal with the spoken word. The classic example of this principle is an opening exercise in first-semester undergraduate linguistics. The captain of a boat, in passing his first mate, somewhat cryptically says to him,

"Ship sails today." The question is, which of two possible things has the captain actually said? As simple a word as *the* can clarify the situation immediately (or in the case of the linguistics student, the not so simple task of learning to point or notate to indicate pitch and accent). Either way, there are two clear possibilities, the correct choice between them hinging on how the captain inflected his voice. Only the first mate, therefore, will ever know with an absolute certainty whether the captain meant, "Ship the *sails* today" or "The *ship* sails today."

We speak today of a *textus receptus*, a received text, as the platform from which we begin our study of the New Testament. The time has come, I suspect, for us to speak in terms of the Received Jesus just as surely and deftly as we accept a Received Lincoln, and for a similar set of reasons. The Received Jesus is the One we have, the One we have from the hands of the forefathers and foremothers of the faith. Despite reams of textural criticism, deconstruction, and redactionist interpretation, the fact is that there is a canon—battered, sometimes miscopied, probably sometimes edited, but still a canon. At each turn of the screw over the centuries, this canon has been validated and revalidated in prayer and faithful discernment. At some point—now, in fact—we must come again to trust the Church as a learning and perceiving construct. Not a denomination or a particularized tradition or a doctrinal division, but the Church, the cumulative and discerning body of Christians no more or less gifted than we who have said, "Here are the words of God. Handle them with fear and wisdom and gratitude."

I was convicted of all these things fairly early in the process of working with Jesus' Sayings. Faith is, by definition, a matter of faith; and by scriptural principle, it requires the cooperative employment of heart, mind, strength, and soul if it is to mature and accomplish its work [I.39; Deut. 6:5]. There is hardly anything new in either of those two statements. The new thing is what happens when one actually accepts the two of them as valid for oneself, which is what I must speak of now. That is, I would be loathe to stop this essay without laying out at least two or three of the things I discovered in focusing, with faith, both my mind and my heart on the Sayings of Jesus. These obviously are things that I had previously failed to assimilate in a lifetime of study of the separate Gospels, and my insights may not seem all that revolutionary or new except to me. Nor do I think I am "right" in what I am about to say. I only mean to say what I have found and what seems at this point in time right to and for me. If my doing so does indeed spark further reflection among readers and the courage to explore what the Sayings mean to them, then that will be all to the good. For it is in the engagement and the pondering and the discovery that faith finds its proper exercise.

The first thing I discovered about Jesus Himself was, like the question of my initial motivation, more mechanical and curious than integral, or so it seemed initially. As I worked to set His words free from all their surrounds, what kept popping up like an annoying cork on otherwise smooth water was a subtle shifting in how He presented. The more I worked, the more the shifting began to seem randomly consistent as well as annoying. What was He doing? Why, for instance, in speaking about defilement, does He say, "Hear me, all of you, and understand: There is nothing outside a person's mouth that by going in can defile, but the things that come out of a person are what defile" [I.32], and then just leave the words there, naked and powerful but opaque and offensive, particularly to legalists and the naively religious?

Why such abruptness? Such near harshness, like a gauntlet thrown down? Why, especially in view of the fact that shortly thereafter He delivers one of the dearest and most patient bits of discourse in the whole of His Sayings? When the disciples ask Him what He has meant by His declaration, He answers, "Then do you also fail to understand? Do you not see that whatever comes into a person from outside cannot defile him or her, for it enters not the heart but the stomach, and goes on out into the sewer? Rather, it is what comes out of a person that defiles; for it is from within, from out of the human heart, that evil intentions come" [II.22].

Yet patient or not, in His obvious concern for these listeners, He also emphasizes the significance of what He is trying to convey by heightening the crudity in how He says it. What He is taking on here, at least on the surface, is Jewish dietary law; but what He is really asserting is a new definition of the human being, one that is part of the substructure of His teaching. We are, in effect, a portal between the Creator and the creation, between that which is outside of space-time and that which is caught within it. Like any other animal, we eat and we defecate. Unlike any other animal, however, we import into creation as well. Such a startling readjustment of perception is fundamental to His instruction. Unlike the crowds, these men and women who are to become His active adherents *must* understand, and the increase in His urgency is made palpable in His language.

Why publicly say of Mary, "Who is my mother? Whoever does the will of my Father in heaven is my brother and sister and mother" [I.28]. Why such apparent cruelty, for it must have stung her? But yet, when in extremis, He says with great tenderness, "Woman, behold your son" and provides for her care [IV.57]. Why the difference, the near-inconsistency of attitude? Why, in a sense, "use" her to dramatically make a point in one situation and reach out to her in tenderest affection and gratitude in another? Why indeed? And then it dawned on me.

Even an amateur psychologist understands that how we present ourselves is always shaped, to some greater or lesser extent, by the audience to whom we are talking and by the role or persona from within which we understand ourselves to be speaking. By the time we are four or five years old, for instance, every one of us interacts verbally with playmates and peers with a vocabulary, syntax, and attitude that are entirely distinct from those we employ in dealing with a sibling, which in turn are distinct from those we use in addressing a parent, which are most definitely distinct from those involved in speaking to a favorite grandparent, all of which are patently distinct from the vocabulary, syntax, and attitude any five-year-old uses when giving a speech at the kindergarten graduation.

There's nothing mysterious about those adjustments. They are instinctive and universally human.

I just had never thought about Jesus being human at
that level, of His being so subject to the same kind of
innate human instincts and qualities that the rest of us
are. Of course He presents and conducts Himself differently in differing situations. Why ever wouldn't He? Once
was the time I would have regarded such a discovery as
close to irreverent and a threat to His godness. Now I
embrace it with a kind of fond gratitude. It was, you
must understand, the first place in the course of this
work that He demanded I let Him out of my precon-
ceptions.

   So I let Him out. I let Him, or His Sayings anyway,
tell me who the personas were or perhaps better said,
what the speaking roles had been. There are—or so it
has seemed to me—five of them. There are the Sayings
that come from His public preaching, those that were
spoken in private instruction, those that were exercised
in His healing dialogue, those said in intimate conversation, and last of all, those He said after His Resurrection.
In each category, the consistency of Jesus of Nazareth's
personality is shaded and shaped by the particularity of
either His audience—public, private, or intimate—or
an activity—healing. His few post-Resurrection Sayings
are shaped by circumstance or, if you will, by translation, for He is no longer human in the mortal sense of
that word.

   I should hasten to say, of course, that there are a
few places where the distinctions by category are not
nearly so clear as they are with most of the Sayings.
Particularly in the Sayings of public teaching and those
of private instruction, there is an occasional blurring of
tone. Interestingly enough, in those cases the Gospelers

themselves often differ about who the listeners were and/or about how personal or intimate the delivery was. Luke, for example, has Jesus speaking the famous "Give, and it shall be given unto you" lines to His disciples, while both Matthew and Mark record these words as having been publicly delivered, which is the category in which I have placed them [I.15]. There is also a place or two where Jesus is presented as speaking alternately to the disciples, to an attendant crowd, and to specific people in that crowd. Even the Sayings themselves read and sound as if He were moving His delivery back and forth from one group to the other.

In Saying I.45, for example, Jesus seems, in both tone and content, to be talking to the disciples when He speaks of the scribes and Pharisees by saying, "Do what they say, but not as they do," just as He is speaking to them when He says, "You are not to be called rabbi, for you have a teacher, and you are all students." Yet without narrative interruption, He swings into His famous invective, "Woe to you, scribes and Pharisees, hypocrites! For you cross sea and land to make a single convert, and you make the new convert twice as much a child of hell as yourselves. Woe to you, scribes and Pharisees, hypocrites!" And so on and so forth.

His railing is interrupted by a lawyer to whom He directly responds, "Woe to you lawyers also! For you load people down with burdens hard to bear." The lawyers gathered in among Jesus' other listeners were of course not barristers in our sense but rather were those who interpreted religious law, and Jesus seems to have had an almost affectionate, or perhaps a mournful, concern for them. As He drew this particular session of teaching to an end, He spoke directly to the lawyer one more time: "And you, woe to you lawyers! For you have taken away the key of knowledge; you did not enter yourselves, and you hindered those who were entering." Those words still stand as some of the most resigned and sorrowful ones ever spoken.

But sorrow, even holy or divine sorrow, must have its counterbalance. It should be no surprise then that in the course of sorting out the Sayings into category, I hit a few moments of being charmed by Jesus and His totally human ways. Every gifted speaker, once he or she has developed a useful metaphor or a telling line, will return to those modes of expression over and over again. Jesus was apparently no different from the rest of us in this. For example, in several settings we hear Him say, "Let those who have ears, hear," or "You brood of vipers!" or more gently, in speaking of children, "Of such is the Kingdom of Heaven." When it seemed that Jesus was, in all probability, purposefully repeating Himself—that He was deliberately pulling out of some previous speech a wording or a concept that He had found to be particularly useful and worth repeating—He left me little choice but to include them. His favorite expressions had to be received not as duplicates or triplicates but as favorites that must be repeated in a gospel of His Sayings as they were in His original speaking. But such moments of easy engagement with the text were short-lived. Within six weeks of beginning the work, I began to be hit by some soul-rattling epiphanies.

The first of them began with a kind of niggling awareness that a disproportionately limited number of Sayings occur during Jesus' acts of healing. In fact, if my count is accurate, there are only twenty-one, almost all of them succinct and having little or nothing to do with the healing itself. Rather, they read now as if much of the time the act of healing became a platform for teaching health of more than just the body. Yet many of us, Christian and otherwise, generally think of Jesus as being almost as much a healer as a teacher. Where, then, given the paucity of words He Himself spoke about healing and healing events, did this sense of heavy emphasis come from? As it turns out, a good deal of it comes not from His words but from the surrounding narrative. Luke's expansive statement, "And that very hour He cured many of infirmities, afflictions, and evil spirits; and to many blind He gave sight," is a good example [Luke 7:21]. Reading such statements, one first suspects that the Gospelers themselves were far more interested in reporting the miracles as proofs of Jesus' divinity than they were in remembering what He said during the process—or at least that was my first conclusion. I was brought up short, however, by an e-mail from a pastor-friend-confrere whom I often consult on such matters. His message jogged my memory about biblical times, while leaving the whole question in a bit of limbo.

What the e-mail so aptly said was, "The ancient historical sources seem to agree that Jesus was a healer and wonder-worker without inferring from that that He was divine, simply because the ancients didn't assume healings could only be done by the gods."

True enough. Ancient history is full of tales about miraculous cures that are attributed in equal proportions to prophets, holy men, emperors, and even a few gifted crones—special or inspired people, in other words, but still basically just human beings. Jesus Himself even pledged to His disciples, "The one who believes in me will also do the works that I do and, in fact, will do greater works than these" [IV.47]. Human beings again.

"But then," the message in front of me said, "all that's debatable. The Asia Minor gang thought Paul was a god when he healed. So it's probably a mixed bag."[3] Wonderful, just wonderful! I still had no idea why there were such effusive references to the healings and why so few words from them were recorded. Then it occurred to me that the most plausible explanation just might be that there were not a lot of words to record. That is, working from the assumption that with the healings as with everything else what was said of importance was by and large what was recorded, one comes to another, more interesting conclusion. For Jesus Himself the healing may always have been servant to something else.

When He speaks later about the events that Luke describes, Jesus certainly acknowledges the healing of the blind, the lame, the deaf, the leprous, and the dead. But He concludes His listing differently. He says, "The lepers are cleansed, the deaf hear, the dead are raised, the poor have good news brought to them. And blessed is anyone who takes no offense at me" [IV.11]. Clearly, to Jesus the business of objective or visible healing is only a part of a larger ministry. Quite possibly, in fact, the healing is not just an act of compassion, but more significantly is a

---

[3] E-mail to the author dated June 11, 2007, from Ken Wilson, senior pastor of the Vineyard in Ann Arbor, Michigan, and district director for the Vineyard Association. Wilson concluded his note by saying, "I just think we use the 'He healed because He was divine' as a dodge to not try it ourselves, so I resist the healing-divinity question. But that's just me."

tool. "Good news," though neither visible nor objectively evident, matters far more than do overt miracles. It would seem, moreover, that there is a strong probability that all of it—healing, resurrecting, and bringing good news—is going to offend, drive away, or grieve many of those who hear Him or hear about Him. Together, they are to winnow out those who can dare the Kingdom from those who cannot.

That is strong language, and it led me to ask, "So, in His general teaching of the Good News, to what does He seem to give the greatest attention? Where in His Sayings was His emphasis?" It's a good question that I had never pondered before—primarily, I suspect, because without seeing the Sayings lined up together as a whole, it would be a difficult question to approach. Certainly it is a question for which there is no unimpeachable answer, even now. But if one looks at the sum total of the teaching Sayings and then asks which theme or subject occurs most frequently, the answer is a startling one—or at least it was startling to me. What Jesus speaks of most often is what we now, in everyday parlance, lump together under the phrase "the End Times."

From childhood on I had been taught—as was indeed true—that the early Church anticipated the imminent end of the world for over a century and conducted itself as if quite literally there would be no tomorrow. At any moment, those early Christians believed, in the twinkling of an eye even, Jesus would return to receive His followers into glory, the Kingdom of God would be established in a new Heaven and earth, and all of the present transient, sin-filled creation would be destroyed. When that cataclysmic event did not occur, or so my Sunday

School instruction went, Christians began gradually to reshuffle their interpretation of the prophetic Sayings. Some held that the Kingdom had already come [I.56] and that, as believers, Christians are to live as if within it rather than by the values of the corrupt, visible world. Others, believing that the Kingdom was being delayed out of mercy, began to evangelize and to emphasize the here and now over the still-to-come. Human conduct within time was what must concern Christians, for godly living here is how we prepare ourselves to be received into an approaching but inevitable Kingdom.

This second line of thought was the one, obviously, that became dominant over the centuries. Certainly it and its corollaries were the ones under which I was formed. I was early shaped to believe that there is a Heaven and there is a Hell, just as there is, or will be, an end to creation and an eventual Judgment Day. Jesus' coming was an act of divine love intended to spare us Hell and grant us Heaven. All of that is orthodox Christian teaching—a little pat, but nonetheless standard pew- or lay-level theology. Or it was standard until the Dead Sea Scrolls and mid- to late-twentieth-century scholarship began to add whole layers of context to the conversation.

The Scrolls were discovered near Qumran by an Arab sheepherder who apparently was merely doing his job when in 1947 he stumbled upon what we now know was part, if not all, of the library of the Essene community. Up to that point, the Essenes had been known to us almost entirely through references to them in historical documents. What the Scrolls reveal, however, is not only the existence of the Essenes as a vibrant religious community, but also a great deal about the apocalypticism that drove them. As a community, they were in truth consumed with end times and had withdrawn from Jewish society because of it. They had ordered their desert community around end-times theology and given themselves over to the maintenance of the writings that recited the signs, causes, and results of apocalypse.

If that were all that the Scrolls could tell us, they would probably have remained safely in the hands of archeologists and historians as scholarly treasures. That was not to be, however, for the Scrolls opened more than the Essenes' apocalypticism. They revealed as well the vast variety and intensity of end-times thinking and concern in first-century or Second Temple Judaism. Suddenly Jesus' teachings about the Eschaton and the Kingdom took on a context that cried out to be an interpretive one.

In reality, it took over a decade for the significance of Qumran even to begin to filter out from the Israeli desert. The Scrolls, like every archeological discovery made in Israel, were tightly controlled and access to them was carefully restricted by Israel's Antiquities Authority. Israeli law forbids the release of all such materials to open viewing or use for fifty years from the date of their discovery. As a result, it was 1997 before the world's commercial media had much access at all to the Scrolls. Independent of legal restrictions was the fact that careful scholars themselves move slowly. It is the nature and virtue of their profession that they do so. In the case of the Scrolls, carefulness also meant that all the things that the scholars who were permitted to work with the Scrolls were discovering had to be vetted by other scholars before it could be discussed in print. Once cleared for print circulation, though, the data had to be reported first in scholarly journals for further vetting. Only then, and very slowly, could they be transmuted into popularized material that would be accessible and comprehensible to nonspecialists. All of which is to say that it took almost the full fifty allotted years for the Scrolls and their revelations to become anything like active components in popular end-time theology and conversation.

Once the popularization of Qumran information had achieved a firm grip on lay American Christianity's attention, the result was almost immediately one of two things: receptive reaction and formidable counterreaction. There was little or no middle ground. Many clergy and, after that, many laity began to revisit Jesus' teachings about the hereafter and to introduce or reintroduce various possibilities for interpreting them. Given that apocalypticism was so clearly a major part of first-century Jewish thinking, perhaps Jesus used those themes as easily accessible metaphors for teaching the people about the necessity for changing their ways in this world. Perhaps Jesus was Himself a persuaded apocalypticist who, under the influence of His fellow Jews just misunderstood end times in the first place. Perhaps Jesus did understand and meant what He said, but metaphorically, not literally. Perhaps Jesus really was striving to be a political force in His world and was urging the people to rebel against Rome. Perhaps He was persuaded that things had gone too far for Rome ever to be overthrown and thus was prophesying the destruction of the Second Temple and the Holy City, not that of the cosmos. Perhaps He was prophesying all of this so that His followers would know years later that the Kingdom was more than Jerusalem and the Temple. Perhaps . . . Perhaps . . . The credible possibilities were at least a half-dozen or so in number, and not one of them was the old, familiar, standard teaching of our pre-Qumran days. But if all the theories were the receptive reaction, they were as nothing in comparison to the counterreaction.

Traditionally persuaded Christians were having none of it. Not one single jot or tittle of contextual interpretation by whatever name one called it was to be admitted anywhere at any time. The backlash and the fury and—let us be honest—the anguish were so great that whole congregations and even denominations began to define themselves in terms of where they stood doctrinally on matters of Armageddon and its attendant ideas. The break on the issue between the "conservative" and "liberal" sides of the Christian camp grew into an abyss, an essentially unbridgeable chasm. Not the least remarkable consequence of the whole thing was the record-shattering sales figures racked up by Christian authors, most of them conservative, writing about what it means to be left behind in the Parousia.

As with any public brouhaha and especially as is true in any brouhaha about religious doctrine, the sides shouting at each other across the chasm became so shrill that content was lost to prejudice. The discussions became arguments that lost clarity and humility early on and assumed instead the methods of personal vilification and disparagement. At some point in that progression I allowed myself to lose interest in the whole matter simply because I deplored the shouting match, and those who were conducting it. In my own defense, I must say that my suspicion is that most run-of-the-mill lay Christians did likewise.

Walking away from the racket led subtly to a new position for me—or us, if indeed it is the case that we were many in number. I simply assumed the drop-back position, that the bulk of the theories and the particulars about all of it—about the Eschaton and the Parousia and eternal damnation, about eschatology in general—were better left as theories than embraced as detailed doctrines. In fact, the common wisdom among me and my kind implied that those who too vigorously make doctrine out of eschatology often are, or can become, weirdos or fundamentalists or both.

Looking back now on my own history, I am not quite sure how, even in the midst of such an uproar, I permitted so huge and blanket a set of assumptions on my part to meld into theological laissez-faire. Suffice it to say, however, that I had, and it did. Not only was I inclined for years to let eschatological details sleep on undisturbed, but I even felt a certain intellectual or social superiority in doing so. Yet, as I worked on the Sayings, it became increasingly clear to me that the early Church had had good reason to think Jesus was telling them that the end was coming, that He would indeed return soon, that there is an actual Hell that can be talked about in the same way as any other place can be talked about, and that a resurrection is coming to all humanity, not just to some elect part of it. Jesus talks about those very things over and over again. Why? And more tellingly, why unless He knew them to be true?

Logic can argue—mine did—that the times in which Jesus spoke and in which the Gospelers wrote were absorbed with and fixated on apocalyptic concerns, as we now know was true. Those concerns, we also now know, had evoked a whole spectrum of interpretations and explanations among the people with whom Jesus lived and taught. It would follow, then, that in such an excited and overwrought context, the teachings about end times would be the ones most likely to be attended to, and therefore the ones most likely to survive in the greatest detail and number when the time came for writing down what He had said. I still have no trouble accepting that argument. In fact, I think it may be exactly what did happen and may well account for the high proportion of end-times Sayings. It does not, however, answer the more foundational question of why He would speak any of those Sayings in whatever quantities if He had not known them to be both true and central to His work.

That question haunted me for days. I made lists of the Sayings that deal with the end and with life after death just to be sure I was correct in my assessment; and then I parsed those Sayings to be sure that they are incontrovertibly words about the hereafter and the yet-to-come, regardless of how one wishes to define or interpret it. They are; and because they are, I could no longer escape them. I could no longer set them apart as belonging in the melee of doctrinal scrimmages and not of concern to my own faith. Nor could I, I discovered, bite down on those half-dozen or so explanations about why Jesus didn't really mean what He said; or if He did, He meant it metaphorically, or politically, or erroneously, or whatever. Instead, and eventually, I had to study the Sayings in prayer, which is the only way I know to pierce through the skin of sacred words and into their meaning or message for me. And what I came out with may be as ordinary and obvious to every other Christian as it has been barrier-breaking for me. What those Sayings share and rest on is the very simple principle that human life cannot end.

Once we are born, we are. Always. Without end or hope of end, we are. Life is eternal; death is eternal. In life or in death, we are without hope of cessation. And if that is not a terrifying thought, I hope never to hear one.

Since 1859 and Darwin's *Origin of the Species*, Western Christianity has been absorbed with evolution and with its perceived threat to the Genesis story of creation. That story records God as saying, "Let us make man in our own image." If humanity was made in the image of God—if we are indeed fashioned *imago dei*—then it cannot also be true that we are descended from some biological forebear whom we hold in common with other species. Or it cannot be true if one assumes that the *imago dei* is two arms, two legs, a head, and a gut, which certainly is how medieval and renaissance thought conceptualized our beginning in the Garden of Eden.

Christians since Darwin (and many before him) have become increasingly content to argue, however, that the image of God that we are is not biological at all and never has been. Correctly read, they say, Genesis tells of God's fashioning a form—in this case, two legs, two arms, a head, and a gut—and thereafter just being a form and only a form until the moment when He breathed His own breath into this particular part of His creation and made of it a living soul. The soul, not the form of its physical presentation within time, is the *imago dei*. So far, so good.

Even as a child I never thought God had arms and legs, much less a head, anyway. As a result, the whole evolution battle has rarely if ever entered into my serious thinking. Instead, it has occupied a place of occasional and casual curiosity about what in the world the ruckus is about. The soul is the image of God, and its infusion into us is the Genesis story. I of course do not know what a soul is and never have, though in this case the deficit is not for want of serious thinking. I do know a number of theories about, or theoretical definitions of, the soul, but I have long since given up on them as well. Yet here, in a sizeable portion of His whole range of Sayings, is Jesus, Son of God, seeming to teach that outside of "now" is "is." And after "now" is done with us and we with it—as soon as space-time's "now" is passed through—everyone of us *is*.

Hell, like the soul, may have been without specific definition or conceptualization for me for lo these many years. I may even have laid it aside as "there" but not really subject to conceptualization. But one cannot do that in working with the Sayings, or I could not. "But I say to you that everyone who is angry with another shall be liable to judgment; whoever insults another shall be in danger of the council; and whoever says, 'You fool!' shall be liable to hellfire," are among the first words of His public preaching [I.7]. So too were, "If your right eye causes you to sin, pull it out and throw it away. It is better to lose one part of yourself, better for you to enter life with one eye and maimed than with two eyes to have your whole body thrown into hell" [I.8]. The story of Lazarus [I.3], the beggar, itself beggars any notion that Hell cannot be graphically defined or described.

In the Sayings—looked at in aggregate and without the distraction of their surroundings, in other words— Hell takes on a kind of definitive concreteness. It also takes on endlessness. For instance, as Jesus is teaching the disciples near the end of His time with them, one of the last things He talks about is the time when He will return in judgment and separate the sheep from the goats. Of the goats, He says, "And these will go away into everlasting punishment, but the righteous into eternal life" [II.49]. Even in His healing monologues, He presses the point. As He is casting out demons, He says to those murmuring around Him, "Whoever speaks a word against the Son of Man will be forgiven, but whoever speaks against the Holy Spirit will not be forgiven, either in this age or in the age to come, for he or she is guilty of an eternal sin" [III.13]. To be endlessly in condemnation rather than in life—that is Hell.

As if to ameliorate or perhaps to console my grasp of such horror, there came a kind of sequel or second part to my prayer conversations. If a part of our being in the image of God is indeed endlessness—if indeed none of us can ever cease to be—would a God not *burn* with the need to make the terms or conditions of endlessness clear to us? Would a God not find some way to come to us with words, even though such clarity might offend, drive away, and grieve?

Salvation and divine love are the core of Christian teaching, of course, but God burning/God yearning are light years (literally) from polysyllabic concepts like sacrificial love or substitutionary death or current theories of atonement. Yet burn, it would seem, was precisely the posture out of which Jesus spoke, just as it is yearning that appears to lead to the intensity and predominance of the eschatological Sayings. You may think otherwise, but for my own part, I find a keening, all-consuming concern far more credible and embraceable than love in the abstract. Jesus was right when He said that these words of His would offend or grieve or drive away many. But those of us who wish to stay, it seems to me, must accept without reservation that What came among us is and was and always will be the Yearning, not a guru.

In the progression of my discoveries, the next was, and still is, a by-product—albeit the loveliest of them—of my wrestling with the Sayings in general and the prophetic end-times ones in particular. In dealing with the eschatological Sayings, I first began to realize I had no "picture" in my head for this offensive, yearning, intense Jesus. I had no image that would or could accommodate the now-obvious emphasis and definitions He placed on the end and the hereafter. A God burning to be fathomed and yet with so grizzly a message was not a Jesus I had ever seen before. Not the teaching white man in full linen gown and red tunic, certainly. Not the defeated peasant dragging a cross up an incline. Not a corpus covered only in a loin cloth and hanging on a crucifix. Not the seated preacher, well-scrubbed and his head aglow, as he addressed also well-scrubbed and worshipful crowds. Certainly not the seated adult male gathering church school children into his protection.

So I had no picture, no mental image, and no way to visualize this new Jesus. That was when it dawned on me that up to that point I had indeed always visualized Jesus. He had always had a seeable form—the seated lover of children, the white-robed and peripatetic teacher, the suffering savior, the haloed rabbi. But we can't "see" words, we have to hear them. And what had happened over the months of sustained and intense work with the words was that Jesus had become "the heard" but no longer "the seen." It sounds ridiculously simple-minded to say that—like a foolish thing for an adult Christian to make very much of. For me, however, it was one of the great personal or private gifts to come out all of the work.

The loss of images happened because of my absorption into the voice. I know that. I know as well that, try as I may, I can never come even close to articulating that process and its results to anybody else, at least not in a crystal-clear way. The nearest I can come is to say that it is most like the difference between looking at the walls and general structure of a room from outside of it and looking at the room from inside of it. The images, the masterpiece paintings and sculptures, even the cheap medals and lithographed prints of Messiah all require a distance. To see is, by definition, to stand back and look. Not so with hearing. To hear is to draw close. To hear is to ride in a stream of words. Ask any lover and he or she will say the same.

Christian Scripture, like the Scripture of Judaism out of which it comes, consistently refers to the "human heart" as a place of knowing and dwelling. Implicit in those teachings is the idea that brain and heart both are organs of perceiving and being, yet they remain patently distinct one from the other. Or the two are distinct and equally informing, if we make two assumptions. First, we must assume that rather than employing a spiritualized or metaphorical use of words, the biblical writers really are referring to some construct emanating from the physical heart in a way that is analogous to the mind as it emanates from the physical brain. Second, given that, we must assume that there is in the human being a means of knowing other than that of the brain. While the first assumption is arguably possible, the second is not easy to assert, especially not in this day of EKGs and MRIs and fMRIs. The notion that the self can receive consciousness from anything other than the brain is as fey as it is untenable. Or it is unless there is indeed a consciousness that is more than mind and in whose image we ourselves are constructed. Were our matter otherwise, why bother to say to us, "'You shall love the Lord your God with all your heart, and with all your soul, and with all your mind, and with all your strength.' This is the first and greatest commandment" [I.39].

It was hardly a surprise to me, of course, when I began to perceive that not only was I no longer imaging Jesus, but also that there had been some kind of shift in where I was "hearing" Him. Goodness only knows, like many another Christian, I have long ago accepted interior "messages" as valid. The surprise was in perceiving experientially that the Sayings, entered prayerfully, are first heard somewhere other than in the mind and only later are transferred to the integrated self, not the other way around. Being forced to acknowledge, in a working, practical way, that somewhere in me there is a second site or organ or means of knowing that led to my realizing that that which it knows and reports is the traffic going in and out of it. Now I realize, of course, that one has only to listen in order to perceive this principle as central to Jesus' teaching:

"For out of the abundance of the heart the mouth speaks. The good person brings good things out of a good treasure of his heart, and the evil person brings evil things out of an evil treasure; for out of the abundance of one's heart does he or she speak" [I.25].

"Blessed are the pure in heart, for they shall see God" [I.4].

"The reason I speak in parables to those outside is that 'seeing, they do not perceive, and hearing, they do not listen, nor do they understand.' With them indeed is fulfilled the prophecy of Isaiah that says:

'You will indeed listen, but never understand,
and you will indeed look, but never perceive.
For this people's heart has grown dull,
and their ears are hard of hearing,
and they have shut their eyes;
so that they might not look with their eyes,
and listen with their ears,
and understand with their hearts and turn—
and I would heal them'" [II.15].

The heart, it would seem, has its own consciousness and knowledge and ways that can be experienced just as the brain's consciousness and knowledge and ways are experienced. They are just not as scientifically measurable at the moment, and may never be. We do know a few things, however. We know that mystical experiences and such more-or-less common things as near-death episodes involve the brain's "shutting down" or "turning off" part of its normal, routine function. Yet specific, conscious recall—often even heightened cognition—is almost unfailingly present after such events. What part of the prophet first receives the prophet's message? What part of the lover first perceives love? What part of us first rejoices in a summer rainbow? Who can answer these things?

Accepting, even cautiously, the possibility of a receptive and cognitively functional heart probably raises a myriad of questions. Only one of them seems accessible here. Accepting the heart as a way of knowing requires a reexamination of what sacred writ is. It forces the question of to whom or to what that holy writ is speaking, to whom or what it is directed.

Because as a faith tradition Christianity has never developed anything close to the gracefulness of Judaism's *Midrash*, the centuries of our history are rife with squabbles over the literalness of the Bible. Few of those centuries have ever been more tendentious and battle-scarred than is our own. While folks who take their Bible literally condemn as religious libertines and Hell-bound those who do not, believers who take their Bible to be metaphorical and evolving condemn the literalists as dangerous citizens and anemic believers.

Neither side of that divide is very attractive, whether to each other or to anybody else looking in. Nor have I ever been comfortable aligning myself with either one. Yet always I have felt myself fumbling when, in trying to present my position on the issue, I claim literal belief in the Bible, "just not in the way that phrase is usually understood." Until the Sayings work came along, I sensed, but for some reason was denied entry into, what I meant. Now I know.

From inside the room, from inside the words, one perceives that staying in the words is more rigorous and blessed than is prowling around outside of them in some kind of effort to see or imagine what they "really mean." They don't mean; they are. And what they are is for both the heart and the mind to assimilate in concord with one another, never separately. This is a perception that at first blush seems deceptively simple, perhaps, but out of it has come what is, for me anyway, one of the most welcome gifts of all. If my pleasure should seem disproportionate, believe me, it is more than proportionate in terms of the discomfort I endured for years before the Sayings work came along.

And the gift? That in addition to the approaches of the literal and the metaphorical camps there is a third way of knowing the Scriptures. There is—for want of a better word—*actualness.* There is interior to Scripture a holiness that is subject neither to literalness nor to metaphorical translation, but rather is the irreducible, ineluctable cohesion of it. The holiness of Scripture is its actualness, its unsplitable state; and conversely, the actual existence or pith or vitality of Scripture is its holiness. That is, by assuming an interior rather than an exterior point of view in considering Scripture, I became persuaded by two things: the bald-faced truth of it and the impossibility of ever, in time, receiving its full meaning. Though I deplore the word, I would even dare to say here that there is no possibility in time of our ever "concretizing" Holy Writ, of ever being able to make so much of an objective "thing" out of it as to be able truly to say, "Ah, here it is!" or "Look! Now I have it." On that basis, I am, as of quite recently, a self-proclaiming dealer in biblical actualness.

It was, as I have said, my unpremeditated slide from imaging to hearing that first exposed me to actualness, both as a third way and as a name for what I had always sensed but not been able to own. The progression from imaging to hearing to becoming a biblical actualist was, in retrospect, fairly direct and went something like this: It is a given that Hebrew Scripture makes quite a thing about no images. The first sections of the Law, in fact, deal with the issue in some detail. As a product of the Enlightenment and Rationalism and Protestant literacy in general, I know that. Second, like most of my tribe, I also had drilled into me from childhood on that the Hebrews were not to make images of God, because representations of God or any part of His creation could lead to idolatry. And as we all know, I was also taught, the early Hebrews lived in very primitive times, among pagan peoples who were prone to the worship of idols. Therefore, because of their having to live in such corrupt and corrupting circumstances, the Hebrews were forbidden to make images of any created thing or of the Creator. Unfortunately, all of this somewhat puerile explanation not only was but still is offered in Christian Education as *an* or *the total* explanation.

There is an old truism in medicine that says once a physician has a name for a disease, he or she is more than halfway along to finding its cure. The same is true of religion and explanations. Once there is an explanation, one is halfway along to defanging and domesticating a religious precept. In the matter of the making of images, the domesticating sketched here had been complete long before I came into this world. As a feat, its complete acceptance had rested for centuries on the premise that enlightened Western Christians are not subject to idolatry, our civilizations being far too advanced for such. And because idolatry and its dangers are the only logical explanation for Moses' prohibitions, then we no longer have reason either to worry about or observe them. There was also the additional, though usually unvoiced, corollary that held that drawing and sculpting images of Jesus was not imaging God, at least not in the Mosaic sense anyway. How could it have been, because Moses could not even have known about Jesus, except, at the greatest stretch, in prophetic theory. Makes perfect sense, doesn't it?

In all fairness, some smaller branches of Western Christianity say, and always have, "No, it doesn't make sense at all, and we will dare no images." The rest of us have gone merrily on our way—and with glorious results. The sacred painting and sculpture of the Renaissance alone would persuade even the stones of the roadway to praise God, just as the sacred painting and sculpture of the Middle Ages had taught the stories of God to an illiterate populous. How then can the biblical injunction against imaging be seen as pertinent always and in all circumstances? For literalists, it must, and centuries of art be damned. For the metaphorical interpreters, yesterday's laws are important as insights into yesterday's problems, but no longer apply to our new day. But for the actualist, I now know, the answer is neither of the above.

The only tenable position for the actualist is that the law still holds and actually cannot be changed; rather, it must be realized fully enough so that its truth is apparent always and everywhere. The error is not in the beauty of our art. The error is that in our making and using art, we forgot—or perhaps scorned—Eastern Christianity's holy insistence on the necessity of distortion in sacred art. Having taken that first step, we next lost, and therefore ceased to teach ourselves, the distinction between the Divine Itself and the time-and-culture-specific images we create from our imagining of the Divine. Such failure plays directly into the apparently inherent tendency of human beings to internalize images, making of them, however subtly, scrims over the presence of God.

The irony in all of this, which I am sure is now apparent to all, is twofold. First, Moses, the poor primitive, was right all along. Second, Jesus was an actualist, not a literalist or a metaphorist. In fact, He routinely took on both of those camps, asserting the presence, interior to Scripture, of what it is and was and is about.

> "Think not that I have come to abolish the law and the prophets; I have come not to abolish them but to fulfill them. For truly I say to you, until heaven and earth pass away, not one jot or tittle will pass from the law until all is accomplished. Indeed, it is easier for heaven and earth to pass away than for one iota of the law to become null and void. Whoever then relaxes one of the least of these commandments and teaches men to do so shall be called the least in the kingdom of heaven, but he who does them and teaches them shall be called great in the kingdom

of heaven. For I tell you, unless your righteousness exceeds that of the scribes and Pharisees, you will never enter the kingdom of heaven" [I.6].

The righteousness of the scribes and Pharisees was of course primarily the sin of literalism. We know that and tend to delight, for example, in how often and deliberately He used the Sabbath for acts of healing or mercy simply because it offended the literalists. By doing so, He gained opportunities to argue for what the law actually says. What it says of the Sabbath is that one must keep it holy. To fulfill, therefore, the center of the commandment is to pursue holiness on the Sabbath, not edicts or derivative principles about it. Those things violate the integrity, which is the integrity or holiness, of the law. But on a few occasions, Jesus also chastises the religious of His day not for being not literal but for being metaphorical instead of actual.

The Sadducees, who taught that there was no resurrection, once came to Jesus with a kind of doctrinal test or trap. They postulated a good woman whose husband dies, leaving her childless. Because humanity is to be fruitful and multiply, Jewish precept taught that in such a situation the deceased husband's next youngest brother must marry his brother's widow. In the Sadducees' hypothetical story, the younger brother did marry her, and then he likewise died, again leaving her without any children. This went on through seven brothers, each of them dying and leaving the widow childless.

People with any sense of humor at all would immediately quip that whatever else the story might prove, it certainly proves that this woman was a very dangerous one to do marital business with. But the Sadducees were on a mission. They were intent on using their story as a way to maneuver Jesus into either agreeing with them that there is no resurrection or committing, to them, the religious sin of contending that there is. So, having postulated their story, they ask Him whose wife the woman will be in the hereafter. His answer is that they are wrong because they have read as metaphorical a portion of Scripture which they should have received as actual.

> "Is not this the reason that you are wrong, because you do not know either the scriptures nor the power of God? . . . as for the dead being raised, have you not read in the Book of Moses what was said to you by God in the story about the bush, how God said, 'I am the God of Abraham, the God of Isaac, and the God of Jacob'? He is not God of the dead, but of the living; you are quite wrong" [I.65].

Perhaps most famously and most directly He asserts the actualness of Scripture in a moment of pure theology, a theology that ran like a wild fire straight through the basic tenets of Second Temple Judaism. The Pharisees and scribes had gathered up stones and surrounded Him, with the express intention of stoning Him to death. His unpardonable offense, they said, was that of blasphemy, for He claimed to be God.

> He says to them, "Is it not written in your law, 'I said, "You are gods"'? If He called those to whom the word of God came 'gods'—and the scripture cannot be denied—how is it you can say that the one whom the Father has sanctified and sent into

the world is blaspheming because I said, 'I am God's Son'? If I am not doing the works of my Father, then do not believe me. But if I do them, even though you do not believe me, believe the works, so that you may know and believe that the Father is in me and I am in the Father" [I.49].

No literalism. None of the embroidery of metaphor. Just the actuality that is the center of the words.

As I look back now on all the things, such as imaging, that have arrested my attention during these months of work, I am keenly aware that most of those ideas are more or less traditionally orthodox ones. Rather than being new or in some sense never before articulated into the canon of Christian thought and exegesis, they have always been there. The problem seems to have been that, for me anyway, they had become more buried in history than visible in the present, more covered in the surroundings than vibrant in the words.

One of the characteristics of age is that it returns us to that from which we came: to long hours of remembering, of recalling, of revisiting. It often returns us as well to the values and moral perceptions of our initial rearing. There were times this past two years when I thought that perhaps that was what was happening to me—times when I wondered if the very orthodoxy of some of what I was perceiving and rejoicing in was not really little more than a return to the comfort of how I had been reared by my devout Presbyterian parents. I think now that the answer to that possibility is both yes and no. That is, I think I have been returned, probably by both age and the intensity of the work itself, to consider again the themes of Jesus' words, not as I once did in my young life as a forming Christian, but as I am now doing as an aging one. Same values, same Sayings and words, same yearning, but a different perspective. All that has changed is that I am old enough now to be surprised again, and I am grateful.

All that having been said, the next surprise may still seem more inane than anything else. The surprise that overtook me gradually, but totally, was that Jesus was a Jew. This is hardly late-breaking news, even for the most protestant Protestants. I can remember a time, however, when that fact was not bandied about quite so blatantly as I have bandied it here. I can even remember when, in the 1980s and 1990s, commercially published books about Jesus of Nazareth as a Jew or Hebrew or Rabbi were just scandalous enough to receive a lot of media attention and enjoy very impressive sales figures. So the idea itself was hardly worthy of being noticed when it first began to intrude. Or it was not worthy until I began to notice not that He was a Jew but that He was flagrantly and assertively a Jew. He went to a lot of trouble not only to make it clear that He was a Jew, but also to ensure that those of us who would hear of Him later by books and word of mouth would understand that His being Jewish was a big part of the deal here. On this subject too, in other words, the Sayings seem disproportionate.

What, to take one example, could be clearer than His words to the Samaritan woman at the well? "You worship what you do not know; we worship what we know, for salvation is from the Jews" [II.2].

Or to the Syro-Phoenician woman, "I was sent only to the lost sheep of Israel. Let the children be fed first, for it is not fair to take the children's food and throw it to the dogs" [III.14].

There is no lack of clarity either in His repeated condemnation of Gentiles and their ways. For instance, "So do not be worried, saying, 'What shall we eat?' or 'What shall we drink?' and do not be of anxious mind. It is the nations of the world that seek after all these things, but your Father already knows that you need them" [I.14].

Nor could anything be more direct than His first commission to the disciples: "Go nowhere among the Gentiles, and enter no town of the Samaritans, but go rather to the lost sheep of the house of Israel" [II.7].

He is, as we know, going to reverse all of these positions. Some of them He will reverse immediately. After maneuvering the Samaritan woman at the well into the admission that she worshiped as her ancestors had done—not in Jerusalem but on a mountain of Samaria—He says, "Woman, believe me, the hour is coming when you will worship the Father neither on this mountain nor in Jerusalem. . . . But the hour is coming, and is now here, when the true worshipers will worship the Father in spirit and truth, for the Father seeks such as these to worship Him. God is spirit, and those who worship Him must worship in spirit and truth" [II.2].

It is to the same woman that He first says of the Messiah, "I who speak to you am He." He says this not to a Jew but to a Samaritan, and one, moreover, into whose face He had just rubbed His Jewishness. Why? Why more or less insult her and her tradition, only to turn minutes later to accept her by honoring her above all His other hearers?

Having called the Syro-Phoenician woman a dog unworthy of sitting at table with Jews, He pivots within two sentences and says to her, "O woman, great is your faith!" He then grants her the benison she seeks, "May it be done for you just as you desire. Go—the demon has left your daughter." Why? There could hardly be a more odious or alienating insult than what He has delivered to her. Why do it if He is only going to turn around and fulfill the very request that occasioned His insult in the first place?

And although over and over again He may have publicly condemned Gentile values and mores, in other situations He not only embraces individual Gentiles but also makes it very clear that it is the ways, not the people, that He is condemning. Thus, in curing the sick servant of a Roman centurion, Jesus not only heals the servant but also affirms His reason for doing so, saying of the Roman, "Truly I say to you, not even in Israel have I found such faith" [III.5].

Scarcely has He uttered those words, moreover, than He turns to those gathered around Him—presumably Jewish—and takes them on: "I tell you, many will come from east and west and will eat with Abraham and Isaac and Jacob and all the prophets in the kingdom of heaven, while you yourselves, the heirs of the kingdom, will be thrust out; for behold, some are last who will be first, and some are first who will be last."

And after the Resurrection, as He issues not His first but His final commission to His followers, He speaks the greatest reversal of all: "Preach the good news to every creature; for those who believe and are baptized will be saved, but those who do not believe will be condemned ... and you will be witnesses to me in Jerusalem, and all Judea and in Samaria, and to the very ends of the earth.... And remember, I am with you always, to the end of the age" [V.6].

There are no accidents with Jesus' Sayings, only a kind of rugged grandeur. There may have been—undoubtedly were—some textural corruption along the way, some paraphrase, some editing; but none of that has managed to distort or obliterate the themes. Once the patterns are excavated, the debris dusting their surfaces is only debris. And Jewishness is a major pattern in the Sayings—Jewishness not as a genetic construct but as a prophetic one; Jewishness as a divinely appointed and ordained human road into space/time for the purpose of completing creation. It took me a while to perceive the presence of that telling difference in what He was saying and doing.

People as living souls are all *imago dei*, but not all peoples and tribes have the narrative, the divine plan, the *institutum dei*, the intention of God. Only to the tribe of Abraham, Isaac, and Jacob has its maintenance been given; and of all narratives, it is the most particular. Fixed like a beamed bridge through time, it may suffer accidents and endure collateral abuse, but it cannot be destroyed. It runs from before Eden to the other side of Apocalypse and is the King's Highway, carrying on itself the caravan of God. And the last obstacle to be tunneled through was, ironically, the embroidered fabric of a temple curtain. With His cry of "It is finished!" [IV.60] the veil that separated the sacred area of the Temple from the Holy of Holies rips from top to bottom. There is no more curtain between God and humankind.

It was indeed finished and the bridge complete. But unless that wonder of construction is well-remarked upon, unless it is pointed out and its route repeatedly traced, unless the intricacies of its engineering are celebrated and the perfection of its execution perceived, then we who travel it are diminished by our own ignorance, and our journey becomes more a labor than a triumph.

There is, in our rational times, a pervasive sensibility that invades every one of us when we deal with religion and, to some extent, with spirituality. Actually, it even explains in part our greater comfort in talking about spirituality than about religion. Not only are we terribly informed these days about the historic bloodiness of religious warfare, but we are also terribly—exquisitely, even—informed about the emotional similarities of religions and the cultural disparities that create the antagonisms among the people who adhere to them. For First World people especially, those similarities and disparities, lumped together as part and parcel of one another, can lead to the assumption that all religions, reduced to their basics, are indeed alike. From that point of view, religion is the god business, no more and no less.

Once one assumes such an intellectual stance, it is an easy and frequently taken step to the next notion: If all religions are fundamentally alike in both substance and methods, then there must be, somewhere out there, really only one god, albeit with many personas or presentations. After that, it logically follows that all the franchises of the god-business chain must be dealing in the same basic stock, although in different types of stores and under circumstances particularized to each vendor's customer base. As with any store, the goods being offered for sale must in some way satisfy a need or offer some improvement to human circumstance. Inasmuch as wisdom is the most visible, useful, and satisfying nonphysical need in life, it is also an easy next step to assume that this generic god's successful emissaries—his deliverymen servicing the respective stores or venues—are basically dealers in wisdom. Or to use our popular terms, they are all yogis or sages or wisdom teachers or social activists or saints or gurus who, by virtue of a common profession, share common cause in their desire to enrich human life for the sake of enriching human life.

Such a line of argument, which became increasingly popular in Western culture during the closing decades of the twentieth century, has not been much challenged over the years since then. But when we actually look at the Sayings of Christianity's deliveryman, one of the boulders we stumble over early on is His aggressive assertion of a singular, specific, and immutable plan that is Jewish by both edict and execution and that endures through, across, and over multiple cultures and eras.

"Before Abraham was, I am" [I.36].

"All authority in heaven and on earth has been

given to me.... Go then and make disciples of all nations" [V.6].

Moreover, Jesus' unrelenting, even offensive, emphasis on His Jewishness gives the lie to any sage-only status that might otherwise ever have attached to Him. Such politically incorrect posturing is not wisdom as we commonly understand it today. For that matter, I suspect it was not very well received by some in His day. But if it is not human wisdom, it is unquestionably accompanied by divine imperative. "Let anyone with ears listen!" He says over and over, and over again [I.29 *ff*]. And to be Christian is to follow that instruction. One is Christian rather than merely moral or religious to the extent that he or she follows Jesus as divine completion. Hardly a new conclusion, but certainly a demanding one whose constant articulation the Sayings militantly demand.

By working the Sayings I have become persuaded of another idea that I think warrants attention here. The problem is that what I have been persuaded of is, if not heretical, then certainly not exactly what I would call widely accepted Christian theology. My even mentioning it may in fact confirm the principle that those who *write about* religion should never try to *do* religion. It is too late, however. I am already convicted and must, for better or for worse, say so.

Judaism has, almost from its beginning, divided its sacred canon into three parts: *Torah, Nevi'im,* and

Ketuvim. Torah—or written *Torah*, at least—is the Pentateuch or first five books of what we Christians call the Old Testament. *Nevi'im*, which is the second part of the *TaNaKh*, or Hebrew Bible, is composed of the books of the Prophets. The third division, *Ketuvim*, is the "Writings," meaning the wisdom literature, the Psalms, the stories of Job and Ruth and Daniel, and so on. In this tripartite approach there is considerable realism, not to mention common sense. Not being Jewish, I cannot know for certain but I have long suspected that these divisions indicate a kind of felt or perceived hierarchy of authority—or if not a hierarchy per se, then an appreciative acknowledgment of the differences in the stature of who delivered which parts into being. What that means is that *Torah* trumps *Nevi'im* every time in proximity and immediacy of contact with God.

I do not mean to suggest that there is some kind of contest—or even that there should be—among divisions of the Jewish Bible. I do mean to say, however, that there is a clear distinction between the revealing of divine plan and the giving of the Law in *Torah* and the words of those who worked either as prophets or thinkers and storytellers to guide the people in the ways of the Law and of God's intention that they had received.

In the same way, it can be argued that the Christian New Testament exists in divisions. Commonly they are seen as the Gospels, the Acts of the Apostles, the Epistles, and the Apocalypse or Revelation. My sense of things, after working with the Sayings, is that it is time for us Christians to rethink the vagueness not only of those divisions but also of the equality of authority we unconsciously assign them. The Gospels—the four canonicals and the first chapter of the Acts—are, so to speak, Christianity's *Torah*. Because they contain the words of the plan realized and of the law fulfilled, they come first in our writings, just as they must come first in our gratitude and our attention. The remaining twenty-seven chapters of the Acts and the collections of letters and studies that follow them are our history and our writings. The Revelation is our prophecy.

What I am suggesting here—and with some trepidation—is that the time may have come in popular Christian conversation for us to speak of the differences in authority between the words of Jesus and those of even His most inspired followers. All of Christian Scripture depends from the Gospels, and whatever comes after must be received through them and in terms of them. We Protestants in particular, with our historic preoccupation with Pauline theology, would do well to remind ourselves of that obvious truth several times a day.

It is the correct and proper business of followers to try to discern the meaning of God's words. Jesus Himself teaches the holiness of that endeavor [II.9]. It is not, however, correct and proper business for followers to discern the meaning of God's words only or equally through the discernment of other followers, even inspired ones, who have preceded them in the process. Better always first to honor and do discernment on the words spoken by God, and thereafter to inhabit—even add to—the historic lines of descent that discernment has subsequently taken.

The New Testament, like the *Tanakh*, is a living thing, not a static one. Its words are the basis for an ongoing but divinely directed revelation. Jesus Himself makes that clear. "I still have many things to say to you, but you cannot bear them now. When the Spirit of truth comes, He will guide you into all truth; for He will not speak on His own authority, but will speak whatever He hears.... I have told these things to you in metaphors. The hour is coming when I will no longer speak to you in figures of speech, but will tell you plainly of the Father" [IV.41] or "I have said these things to you while I am still with you. But the Comforter and Advocate, the Holy Spirit, will teach you everything, and remind you of all that I have said to you" [IV.48].

The beating heart of that revelation, as any biblical actualist will tell you, is in the Gospels, not in the epistles or the history or the prophecy. It is the Gospels we must enter first if we are even to try to understand all that has come after them, and continues to come, even to the end of the Age. Amen.

The Words of Jesus compilation is the second time I have crossed territorial lines and presumed to do religion. The first was some years ago, when I began the continuing work of compiling prayer manuals for use in the keeping of the hours or, as it is sometimes called, for use in the observing of the daily offices. I rejoiced, and continue to rejoice, in that work, even as I do in this. I have, however, been at the business of prayer books longer than I have been compiling the words of Jesus. I have certainly been at it long enough to know that there is a downside to doing religion.

To open any part of one's faith, especially its prayers and holy words, to intense scrutiny is to know, even before the fact, that some things are going to change as a result. Some beloved concept will be slaughtered. Some startling and aberrant truth will push to the surface, making a rift in an otherwise smooth fabric of belief. Some treasured consolation will be snatched away as less than mature. From time to time, such may prove to be the case for anyone who works prayerfully with the Sayings.

I choose the words *work* and *prayerfully* with particular care. The Books of Sayings which follow here are not to be read in the same way as one usually reads a Bible. Narrative in form, the Bible's messages are packaged in the cushioning of verbal surrounds. Not so the Sayings. Lacking almost all of that protective pacing, the Sayings often exhibit the sleek starkness of a stiletto seeking a target. Those who enter them do well, therefore, to go in with prayerful heart and mind. Likewise, those who enter would do well to enter only one—rarely more than two—Sayings at a time. We Christians are fond of the term *lectio divina*, a medieval name for the practice of savoring a section of Scripture slowly, thoughtfully, prayerfully—for "working" at it in small pieces, in other words. The practice of holy reading has never been more appropriate, however, than it will prove to be in studying the Sayings.

One other thing about the Sayings themselves probably warrants a mention here. As our Lord Himself observed, it is by our words that we are known. They are both our ultimate action and also our most immutable expression of self. Jesus is no different from the rest of us in this regard. The Jesus who reveals Himself here is a fully integrated personality, but that personality is not as unreservedly open in some venues as in others. Logically, any Sayings gospel of the words of Jesus would commence, as this one does, with the Sayings of His public instruction or preaching. But predictably it is not His public persona that carries us closest to His center. Rather, He is most self-revelatory and open to us in Book Two—in His words of private instruction, or so it seems to me. Talking there with those whom He has chosen and who are to carry forth His Good News after His Ascension, He has great need to reveal who and what and why He is in human form. As a result, beginning the study of His Sayings with Book Two instead of Book One makes psychological, if not logical, sense, and I would suggest the Private Instructions as the best place to begin.

Regardless of how one chooses to begin working with the Sayings, however, the process can be humiliating at times, which is not the same as humbling, though presumably the former leads to the latter eventually. It is also exhausting. In the long hours between losing something that had been comfortably established and receiving a more blessed replacement, the heart and mind know torment, and fear—not of loss but of change; fear that perhaps there will be no bridge across the abyss this time, that always there will be only the edge and never the knowing again; fear that the soul will sin beyond redemption even in journeying along such roads of meditation; fear that there will not be sufficient energy or grace to continue; fear. . . .

For those who, like me, believe that there is not only a God but also an *institutium dei*, those fears are very real and very present. For some who look at the Sayings of Jesus there will be no shock of possibility, no knocking at the old barricades by new insights. So be it. For others, it will not be so. For them it will be, as it has been and is for me, an arduous entering. It is for such as you and me that I pray. It is also for such as you and me, I think, that some months ago I was given the strangest of concepts, that of "a terrible sufficiency."

When the words came, and despite the fact I could not immediately pierce and receive them, I knew them to be a promise and the walking stick necessary for the journey. I mention this here because I think "a terrible sufficiency" comes as a gift to all of us who dare. I also think it is and was what Julian of Norwich understood when she knew in meditation that "sin is behovely, but all shall be well, and all shall be well, and all manner of things shall be well."

That is enough. That is a terrible sufficiency.

A Gospel of
the Sayings
of Our Lord

The Words of Public Teaching

1 The opening proclamation

Jesus said, "The time is fulfilled, and the Kingdom of God is at hand. Repent, and believe in the good news."

2 The opening statement of mission and of His place in Scripture

Jesus, when He was asked to read from the book of Isaiah in Sabbath services, opened to the words, "The Spirit of the Lord is upon me, because he has anointed me to preach good news to the poor. He has sent me to proclaim release to the captives and recovering of sight to the blind, to set at liberty those who are oppressed, to proclaim the acceptable year of the Lord," and said to those gathered there, "Today this scripture has been fulfilled in your hearing.

"Doubtless you will quote to me this saying, 'Physician, heal yourself; what we have heard you did at Capernaum, do here also in your own country.' But truly I say to you that no prophet is without honor except in his own country. For consider, there were many widows in Israel in the days of Elijah, when the heavens were shut up for three years and six months, when there came a great famine over all the land. Now, Elijah was sent to none of them except to Zarephath in the land of Sidon, to a woman who was a widow. And there were likewise many lepers in Israel in the time of the prophet Elisha, but none of them was cleansed except Naaman the Syrian."

3   The relationship between Father and Son, and with Their work

Jesus said, "I tell you most emphatically that the Son can do nothing of himself, but only what he sees the Father do; for whatever He does, the Son does in like manner. The Father loves the Son and shows him all things that He himself is doing; and He will show him greater works than these, so that you may marvel.

"Indeed, just as the Father raises the dead and gives them life, so also the Son gives life to whomever he wishes. The Father judges no man or woman, but rather has given all judgment over to the Son, in order that all should honor the Son just as they honor the Father. Anyone who does not honor the Son does not honor the Father who sent him. Truly, I tell you, anyone who hears

my word and believes in Him who sent me has eternal
life, and does not come into judgment, but has passed
from death to life. I do not judge anyone who hears my
words and yet does not keep them, for I came not to judge
the world, but to save the world. Anyone who rejects me
and does not receive my words already has a judge; on
the last day, the words I have spoken will serve as judge.
For I have not spoken on my own, but the Father has
given me a commandment about what to say and what to
speak, and I know His commandment is eternal life. What
I speak, therefore, I speak just as the Father has spoken.

"I tell you in truth that the hour is coming, and
now is, when the dead will hear the voice of the Son
of God, and those who hear will live; for as the Father
has life in Himself, so He has granted the Son also to
have life in Himself; and He has given him authority
to execute judgment, because he is the Son of Man. Do
not be amazed at this; for the hour is coming when all
who are in their graves will hear his voice and will come
forth—those who have done good, to the resurrection of
life, and those who have done evil, to the resurrection
of condemnation.

"I myself, of myself, can do nothing. As I hear, I
judge; and my judgment is fair, because I do not seek to
do my own will, but the will of Him who sent me. If I
testify about myself, then my testimony is not true. But
there is another who bears witness to me, and I know that
his witness about me is true. You have sent messengers to
John, and he has testified to the truth. Yet I do not receive
affirmation from man, but rather, I say these things so
that you may be saved. John was a burning and shining
lamp, and you were willing to rejoice for a while in his

light. But I have a greater witness than John's; for the works that the Father has given me to complete, the very works that I am doing, testify on my behalf that the Father has sent me. And the Father who sent me has Himself testified on my behalf. You have neither heard His voice nor seen His form, and you do not have His word abiding in you, because you do not believe him whom He has sent. You search the scriptures because you think that in them you have eternal life, and these are they that testify of me; yet you are unwilling to come to me that you might have life.

"I do not receive honor from men; but I know that you do not have the love of God in you. I have come in my Father's name, and you do not accept me; but if another comes in his own name, him you will accept. How can you believe when you accept honor from one another and do not seek the glory that comes from the one who alone is God? Do not think that I will accuse you before the Father! Your accuser is Moses, on whom you have set your hope. If you believed Moses, you would believe me, for he wrote about me. But if you do not believe what he wrote, how will you believe what I say?"

4 The Blessings and the Beatitudes

Jesus said, "Blessed are the poor in spirit, for theirs is the kingdom of heaven. Blessed are those who mourn, for they shall be comforted. Blessed are the meek, for they shall inherit the earth. Blessed are you who are hungry now, for you shall be satisfied. Blessed are those who hunger and thirst for righteousness now, for they shall be satisfied. Blessed are you who weep now, for you shall laugh and be comforted. Blessed are you who hunger and thirst for righteousness, for you shall be satisfied. Blessed are the merciful, for they shall obtain mercy. Blessed are the pure in heart, for they shall see God. Blessed are the peacemakers, for they shall be called sons of God. Blessed are those who are persecuted for righteousness' sake, for theirs is the kingdom of heaven. Blessed are you when men revile you and persecute you and exclude you and utter all kinds of evil against you falsely on my account. Rejoice in that day! Leap for joy and be glad, for your reward is great in heaven, for so their fathers persecuted the prophets who were before you.

"But woe to you who are rich, for you have received your consolation. Woe to you who are full now, for you will be hungry. Woe to you who are laughing now, for you will mourn and weep. Woe to you when all speak well of you, for that is what their ancestors did to the false prophets.

"But I say to you that hear, Love your enemies, do good to those who hate you, bless those who curse you, and pray for those who persecute you."

5 The description of those who can follow Him

Jesus said, "You are the salt of the earth. Salt is good, and every one will be salted with fire. But if the salt has lost its savor, how can it become salty again? Indeed, it is no longer good for anything except to be thrown out, trampled down, walked on. Let him who has ears, listen: Have salt in yourselves, and be at peace with one another.

"You are the light of the world. A city set upon a hill cannot be hid. Nor do men light a lamp and then put it under a bushel basket or under a bed, but rather on a lamp stand and it gives light to all the house. Let your light so shine before men that they may see your good works and glorify your Father who is in heaven. For there is nothing hidden, except to be made manifest, nor is anything secret, except that it may be made known and come into the light. If any man has ears to hear, let him hear."

6   The place of the Law in His Kingdom

Jesus said, "Think not that I have come to abolish the law and the prophets; I have come not to abolish them but to fulfill them. For truly I say to you, until heaven and earth pass away, not one jot or tittle will pass from the law until all is accomplished. Indeed, it is easier for heaven and earth to pass away than for one iota of the law to become null and void. Whoever then relaxes one of the least of these commandments and teaches men to do so shall be called the least in the kingdom of heaven; but he who does them and teaches them shall be called great in the kingdom of heaven. For I tell you, unless your righteousness exceeds that of the scribes and Pharisees, you will never enter the kingdom of heaven."

7   The correct interpretation of the Law and its application

Jesus said, "You have heard that it was said to those of old, 'You shall not murder; and whoever murders shall be liable to judgment.' But I say to you that everyone who is angry with another shall be liable to judgment; whoever insults another shall be in danger of the council; and whoever says, 'You fool!' shall be liable to hellfire. So if you are offering your gift at the altar and there remember that someone has something against you, leave your gift there before the altar and go first and be reconciled with your brother or sister, and then come and offer your gift."

8 New ways of living and being for citizens of His domain

Jesus said, "You have heard that it was said, 'You shall not commit adultery.' But I say to you that everyone who looks at another lustfully has already committed adultery in his or her heart. So if your right eye causes you to sin, pull it out and throw it away. It is better to lose one part of yourself, better for you to enter life with one eye and maimed than with two eyes to have your whole body thrown into hell. And if your right hand causes you to sin, cut it off and throw it away. It is better to lose that one part of your body, better for you to enter life with one hand and maimed than to have two hands and have the whole of you to be thrown into eternal fire. And if your foot causes you to sin, cut it off. It is better for you to enter life lame than to have two feet and be thrown into the abyss where the worm does not die and the fire is never quenched.

"Why do you not judge for yourselves what is right? As you are on your way to go before the magistrate, make friends quickly with your adversary lest he or she hand you over to the judge, and the judge to the authorities, and you end up in jail; for truly I say to you that you will not escape from there until you have paid out your last penny.

"And again you have heard that it was said to those of old, 'You shall not swear falsely, but shall perform to the Lord whatever it is you have sworn.' But I say to you do not swear at all, either by heaven, for it is the throne of God, nor by the earth, for it is His footstool, nor by Jerusalem, for it is the city of the Great King. And do not swear by your own head, for you cannot make one hair on it white or black. But let your yes be yes and your no simply no. Anything more than that comes from the evil one.

"You have heard that it was said, 'An eye for an eye and a tooth for a tooth.' But I say to you do not resist evil. If anyone strikes you on the right cheek, offer to him the other as well; and if anyone wants to sue you and take away your tunic, let him have your cloak also. And with whoever is compelling you to go a mile, go two. Give to every one who begs from you; don't turn away from someone who is seeking to borrow from you; and from anyone who has taken your property, do not ask for its return."

9   First public statement on the place of love in human conduct

Jesus said, "You have heard that it was said, 'You must love your neighbor and hate your enemy.' But I say to those of you hearing me, Love your enemies, bless those who curse you, do good to those who hate you, and pray for those who mistreat, spitefully use, or even persecute you, that you may be sons and daughters of your Father in heaven; for He makes his sun to rise on the evil and on the good, and sends His rain on the just and the unjust. For if you love those who love you, what reward or credit should you have from that? Don't even the tax collectors do that? Don't even sinners love those who love them? And if you greet your friends only and if you do good only to them, what are you doing any differently from what others also do? And if you lend only to those from whom you expect to receive a return, what praise is there for you in that? Even sinners lend to sinners in order to receive as much again. Indeed, lend, expecting nothing in return, and your reward will be great, and you will be sons and daughters of the Most High; for He is kind to the ungrateful and the selfish. Yes, be merciful and compassionate even as your Father is merciful and compassionate. You, therefore, shall be perfect, just as your Father in heaven is perfect."

10   First instruction specifically on religious practice

Jesus said, "Beware of doing good deeds in front of other people in order to be seen by them, for then you will have no reward from your Father who is in heaven. In the same way, when you give alms and charitable gifts, do not sound a trumpet before you as the hypocrites do in the synagogues and public streets so that they will be praised by others. Truly I tell you, they have their reward. But when you give alms, don't even let your left hand know what your right hand is doing, so that your good deeds may be secret; and your Father who sees in secret will reward you.

"And when you pray, you must not be like the hypocrites, for they love to stand and pray in the synagogues and at the street corners in order that they may be seen by other people. Truly I say to you that they have their reward. But when you pray, go into your room and shut the door and pray to your Father who is in secret; and your Father who sees in secret will reward you.

"And in praying, do not heap up empty repetitions as Gentiles do, because they think they will be heard for their many words. Don't be like them in that, for your Father knows what you need before you ask him.

"Pray, therefore, in this way: 'Our Father in heaven, may your name be hallowed. May your kingdom come and your will be done on earth, as it is in heaven. Give us each day our daily bread; and forgive us our debts as we forgive our debtors, for we ourselves forgive those indebted to us. And do not lead us into temptation, but rescue us from the evil one; for yours is the kingdom, and the power, and the glory, forever. Amen.

"For if you do forgive others their trespasses, your heavenly Father will also forgive you; but if you do not forgive others, neither will your Father forgive your trespasses.

"Now then, when you fast, do not look dismal like hypocrites do, for they disfigure their faces in order to show others that they are fasting. Truly I tell you, they have received their reward. But when you fast, put oil on your head and wash your face, so that your fasting may be seen not by other people but by your Father who is in secret; and your Father, who is the one who sees in secret, will reward you."

11   Instruction about the role of looking and seeing in the lives of the faithful

Jesus said, "The eye is the lamp of the body. So, if your eye is sound, your whole body will be full of light; but when your eye is unhealthy, your whole body is full of darkness. Be careful, therefore, lest the light in you be darkness.

"Now if the light in you is darkness, how great is the darkness! But if your whole body is full of light, having no part dark, it will be wholly bright, as when a lamp with its rays gives you light."

12   First instruction on wealth and the spiritual dangers of possessions

Jesus said, "Do not store up for yourselves treasures on earth, where moth and rust consume and where thieves break in and steal; but sell your possessions and give alms, thereby both providing yourselves with purses that do not grow old and also storing up for yourselves treasures in heaven that will not fail, where neither moth nor rust consumes and where thieves cannot break in and steal. For where your treasure is, there your heart will be also.

"No one can serve two masters; for either he will either hate the one and love the other, or he will be devoted to the one and despise the other. You cannot serve God and money."

13   First recorded parable—a teaching about wealth and possessions

Jesus said, "The land of a rich man had yielded an abundance, and he thought to himself, 'What should I do, for I have no room left to store my crops?' Then he said, 'I will do this: I will pull down my barns and build larger ones, and there I will store all my crops and my goods. And I will say to my soul, Soul, you have many goods laid up for many years; take your ease, eat, drink, be merry.' But God said to him, 'Fool! This night your soul will be demanded of you. And then these things you have prepared, whose will they be?' So it is with those who store up treasures for themselves but are not rich toward God."

14   Temporal anxiety as a spiritual and religious danger

Jesus said, "I tell you, therefore, not to be anxious about your life, what you shall eat, or about your body, what you shall wear. For life is more than food and the body more than clothing. Consider the ravens and all the other birds of the air: they neither sow nor reap, they have neither storehouse nor barn, and yet God feeds them. Of how much more value are you than the birds! And which one of you by worrying can add even a day to your span of life? If then you are not able to do so small a thing as that, why do you worry about what you shall wear or any of the rest of it?

"Consider the lilies of the fields, how they grow: they neither toil nor spin; yet I tell you, even Solomon in all his glory was not clothed like one of them. But if God so clothes the grass of the field, which is alive today and tomorrow is thrown into the oven, how much more will he clothe you, you of little faith!

"So do not be worried, saying, 'What shall we eat?' or 'What shall we drink?' and do not be of anxious mind. It is the nations of the world that seek after all these things, but your Father already knows that you need them. Therefore do not be concerned about tomorrow; tomorrow will be concerned with its own affairs. Let each day's troubles be sufficient for that day. Do not be fearful, little flock, for it is the Father's pleasure to give you the kingdom. Strive, therefore, for God's kingdom, and these things will be given you as well."

15   The dangers of judgmentalism in human affairs

Jesus said, "Do not judge, and you will not be judged; do not condemn, and you will not be condemned. Forgive, and you will be forgiven; give, and it will be given to you; for with the judgment you pronounce, you will be judged, and the measure you give will be the measure you get back.

"Pay attention to what and how you hear; the measure you give will be the measure you receive, and still more abundance will be given you. For to those who have, more will be given; and from those who have nothing, even what they think they have will be taken away.

"Why do you see the speck in your neighbor's eye but do not notice the log in your own eye? Or how can you say to your neighbor, 'Friend, let me take out the speck in your eye,' when you do not even see the plank in your own eye? You hypocrite, first take the plank out of your own eye, and then you will see clearly enough to take the speck out of your neighbor's eye."

16 Counterbalancing admonition about discernment

Jesus said, "Do not give what is holy to dogs; and do not throw pearls before swine, because they will trample them under foot and then turn and maul you."

17 The first promise

Jesus said, "Ask, and it will be given to you; search, and you will find; knock, and the door will be opened for you. For everyone who asks receives, and everyone who searches finds, and for everyone who knocks, the door will be opened.

"Is there anyone among you who, if your child asks for bread, will give a stone? Or if your child asks for a fish, will give a snake? Or for an egg, will instead give a scorpion? If you then, who are villainous, know how to give good gifts to your children, how much more will your Father in heaven give good things to those who ask Him!"

18 The summary of the Law and the Tradition

Jesus said, "As you wish others to do to you, so do you to them; for this is the law and the prophets."

19   Concerning the winnowing of the righteous from the unrighteous

Jesus said, "Enter through the narrow gate and strive to enter the narrow door; for the gate is wide and the path is easy that leads to destruction, and there are many who take it. But the door is narrow and the pathway is hard that leads to life, and there are few who find it. Indeed, many, I tell you, will seek to enter and not be able."

20   The proper method for assessing religious leaders

Jesus said, "Beware of false prophets, who come to you in sheep's clothing but inwardly are ravenous wolves. You will know them by their fruits.

"Are grapes gathered from thorns, or figs from a bramble bush? Likewise, a good tree bears good fruit, but every bad tree bears bad fruit. A good tree cannot bear bad fruit, nor can a bad tree bear good fruit; and every tree that does not bear good fruit is cut down and thrown into the fire. In the same way, a good person out of the good treasure of his or her heart produces good, and the evil person out of his or her evil treasure produces evil; for out of the abundance of the heart the mouth speaks. Thus you will know them by their fruits."

21   The primacy of the Father's will over all religious forms

Jesus said, "Why do you call me, 'Lord, Lord,' and not do what I tell you? Not everyone who says to me, 'Lord, Lord,' will enter the kingdom of heaven, but only the one who does the will of my Father in heaven.

"On that day many will say to me, 'Lord, Lord, did we not prophesy in your name, and cast out demons in your name, and do many deeds of power in your name?' Then I will declare to them, 'I never knew you; I do not know where you come from. Go away from me, you evildoers, and depart from me, all you workers of iniquity.'"

22   A parable about enacted and embodied faith

Jesus said, "Everyone then who comes to me and hears these words of mine and acts on them, I will show you what he or she is like. That person will be like a wise one who, building a house, dug deep and laid the foundation upon solid rock. The rain fell, the floods came, and the winds blew and beat on that house, and the streams broke against it; but it could not be shaken. It did not fall, because it had been founded on rock.

"And everyone who hears these words of mine and does not act on them will be like a foolish person who built a house on sand and ground without a foundation. The rain fell, and the floods came, and the winds blew and beat against that house, and the streams broke against it; and it immediately fell. Great was the ruin of that house and great was its fall!"

23   John the Baptizer as fulfillment of prophecy

Jesus, in speaking to the Pharisees about John the Baptizer, said, "You are those who justify yourselves in front of other people, but God knows your hearts. For what is honored among humankind is abomination in God's sight.

"What, then, did you go out into the wilderness to look at? A reed blown about by the wind? What then did you go out to see? Someone dressed in elegant clothes? Look, those who wear soft robes are in the palaces of kings. What then did you go out to see? A prophet? Yes, I tell you, and more than a prophet. This is the one about whom it is written: 'See, I am sending my messenger ahead of you, who will prepare your way before you.'

"Truly I tell you, among those born of women no one has arisen greater than John the Baptizer; yet the least person in the kingdom of heaven is greater than he.

"The law and the prophets were until John. Since then, the good news of the Kingdom of God is preached; but from the days of John the Baptizer until now, the kingdom of heaven has suffered violence, and the violent take it by force. For all the prophets and the law prophesied until John came; and if you are willing to accept it, he is Elijah who is to come.

"Let anyone with ears listen:

But to what will I compare this generation?
They are like children sitting in the marketplaces
and calling to one another,
'We piped for you, and you did not dance;
we wailed, and you did not mourn.'

"For John came neither eating nor drinking, and they say, 'He has a demon'; the Son of Man came eating and drinking, and they say, 'Look, a glutton and a drunkard, a friend of tax collectors and sinners!' Yet wisdom is vindicated by her offspring and her deeds."

24   The call to rest in submission

Jesus said, "Come to me, all you that are weary and are carrying heavy burdens, and I will give you rest. Take my yoke upon you, and learn from me; for I am gentle and humble in heart, and you will find rest for your souls. For my yoke is easy, and my burden is light."

25   The role of words in the soul's life and eternity

Jesus said, "Either make the tree good and its fruit good, or else make the tree bad and its fruit bad; for a tree is known by its fruit. You brood of vipers! How can you speak good things when you are evil? For out of the abundance of the heart the mouth speaks. The good person brings good things out of a good treasure of his heart, and the evil person brings evil things out of an evil treasure; for out of the abundance of one's heart does he or she speak. I tell you, on the day of judgment you will have to give an account for every careless word you utter; for by your words you will be justified, and by your words you will be condemned."

26   The first prophecy concerning death and Resurrection

Jesus said, "It is an evil and adulterous generation that asks for a sign, but no sign will be given to it except the sign of the prophet Jonah. For as Jonah became a sign to the men of Ninevah, so will the Son of Man be to this generation; just as Jonah was three days and three nights in the belly of the sea monster, so for three days and three nights the Son of Man will be in the heart of the earth. The people of Nineveh will rise up at the judgment with this generation and condemn it, because they repented at the proclamation of Jonah, and see, something greater than Jonah is here! The queen of the South will rise up at the judgment with this generation and condemn it, because she came from the ends of the earth to listen to the wisdom of Solomon, and see, something greater than Solomon is here!"

27 Concerning occupation by unclean spirits

Jesus said, "When the unclean spirit has gone out of a person, it wanders through waterless regions looking for a place to be at rest, but it finds none. Then it says, 'I will return to my house from which I came.' When it comes back, it finds that spot empty, swept, and put in order. Then it goes and brings in seven other spirits more wicked than itself, and they enter and live there; and the last state of that person is worse than the first. So will it be also with this evil generation."

28 The proper definition of family

Jesus, upon being told that His mother and siblings were in the crowd and desired His attention, said, "Who are my mother and my brothers? These with me are my mother and my brothers! My mother and my brother are those who hear the word of God and do it. And whoever does the will of my Father in heaven is my brother, and sister, and mother."

29   The parable of the sower and the seed

Jesus said, "Listen! A sower went out to sow. And as he sowed, some of the seeds fell on the path, and birds came and ate them up. Other seeds fell on rocky ground, where there was not much soil, and they sprang up quickly, because they had no depth of soil. But as soon as the sun rose, they were scorched; and because they had no root, they withered away. Other seeds fell among thorns, and the thorns grew up and choked them. Other seeds fell on good soil and brought forth grain, some a hundredfold, some sixty, some thirty. Let anyone with ears listen!"

30   Teaching the crowds at Capernaum

Jesus, speaking to the crowds that had followed Him to Capernaum, said, "I tell you that you are looking for me, not because you saw signs but because you got your fill of bread to eat. Do not work for food that perishes but for the food that endures for eternal life, which the Son of Man will give you. For it is he on whom God the Father has set His seal."

Jesus, when they asked Him how they could do the work of God, said, "This is the work of God, that you believe in him whom He has sent."

Jesus, when the crowd asked Him for a sign of His authenticity and cited Moses' having given manna from heaven as a sign of his authority, said, "Believe me when I tell you, it was not Moses who gave you the bread from heaven, but it is my Father who gives you the true bread from heaven. For the bread of God is he who comes down from heaven and gives life to the world."

Jesus, when the people then asked Him to give them such bread, said, "I am the bread of life. Whoever comes to me will never be hungry, and whoever believes in me will never be thirsty. But I have already said to you that you have seen me and yet believe not. All that the Father gives me will come to me, and anyone who comes to me I will never drive away; for I have come down from heaven, to do not my own will but the will of Him who sent me. And this is the will of the Father who sent me, that I should lose nothing of all that He has given me but should raise it up on the last day. This is indeed the will of my Father, that everyone who sees the Son and believes in him may have eternal life; and I will raise them up on the last day."

Jesus, when the crowd was scandalized by His words and claims, said, "Do not murmur among yourselves. No one can come to me unless he or she is drawn by the Father Who sent me; and I will raise that person up on the last day. It is written in the prophets, 'And they shall all be taught by God.' Everyone, therefore, who has heard and learned from the Father comes to me. Not that anyone has seen the Father except the one who is from God; he has seen the Father. Very truly, I tell you, whoever believes has eternal life.

"I am the bread of life. Your ancestors ate the manna in the wilderness, and they died. This is the bread that comes down from heaven, so that one may eat of it and not die. I am the living bread that came down from heaven. If anyone eats of this bread, he or she will live forever; and the bread that I will give for the life of the world is my flesh."

Jesus, when the crowds disputed among themselves about His meaning, said, "Verily, verily, I say to you, unless you eat the flesh of the Son of Man and drink his blood, you have no life in you. Those who eat my flesh and drink my blood have eternal life, and I will raise them up on the last day; for my flesh is food indeed and my blood is true drink. Those who eat my flesh and drink my blood live in me, and I in them. Just as the living Father has sent me, and I live because of the Father, so whoever eats me will live because of me. This is the bread that came down from heaven, not like that which your fathers and mothers ate, and died. But the one who eats this bread shall live forever."

31   On religiosity as a rejection of God

Jesus, speaking to the Pharisees and scribes, said, "And why do you break the law of God for the sake of your tradition? Indeed, you have a fine way of rejecting the commandments of God in order to keep your own traditional rules, which you hand on. God said, 'Honor your father and your mother,' and, 'Whoever speaks evil of father or mother must surely die.' But you say that whenever one says to father or to mother, 'Whatever support you might have had from me is Corban, that is, given to God as an offering,' then that person need not honor either father or mother. So, for the sake of your tradition, which you have handed down, you render void the word of God, and many other such things you do. You hypocrites! Well did Isaiah prophesy about you when he said:

> 'This people honors me with their lips,
> but their hearts are far from me;
> in vain do they worship me,
> teaching human precepts as doctrines.' "

32 The source of personal defilement

Jesus said, "Hear me, all of you, and understand: There is nothing outside a person's mouth that by going in can defile, but the things that come out of a person are what defile."

33 Assertion of His divine commission

Jesus said, "My teaching is not mine but His Who sent me. If anyone resolves to do the will of God, he or she will know whether it is from God or whether I am speaking on my own. Anyone who speaks on his own seeks his own glory; but the one who seeks the glory of him who sent him is true, and there is no unrighteousness in him.

"Did Moses not give you the law? Yet not one of you keeps it. Why are you looking for an opportunity to kill me? I performed one work, and all of you are astonished. Moses gave you circumcision (it is, of course, not from Moses but from the patriarchs), and you circumcise a man on the Sabbath. If a man receives circumcision on the Sabbath in order that the law of Moses may not be broken, are you angry with me because I healed a man's whole body on the Sabbath? Do not judge by appearances, but judge with righteous judgment.

"You know me, and you know where I am from. I have not come of my own self. But the one who sent me is true, and you do not know Him. I know Him, because I am from Him, and He sent me. I shall be with you a little while longer, and then I am going to Him who sent me. You will search for me but you will not find me; and where I am you cannot come."

34   On judging the sins of others

Jesus, when they brought to Him a woman caught in adultery and asked if they should stone her according to the Law, said, "Let him who is without sin cast the first stone."

Jesus, when they had all one by one left, said, "Woman, where are your accusers? Has no one condemned you?"

Jesus, when she told Him that none had accused her, said, "Neither do I condemn you. Go and sin no more."

35   The assertion of His primal and fundamental nature

Jesus, to the crowd gathered around Him in the Treasury of the Temple, said, "I am the light of the world. Whoever follows me shall not walk in darkness but will have the light of life. The light is with you for a little longer. Walk while you have the light, so that the darkness will not overtake you.

"Even if I testify on my own behalf, my testimony is true because I know where I have come from and where I am going, but you do not know where I came from or where I am going. You judge according to human standards; I judge no one. And yet, if I do judge, my judgment is true, for I am not alone, but I am with the Father Who sent me. In your law it is written that the testimony of two witnesses is valid. I am one who bears witness of myself, and the Father Who sent me bears witness to me. You know neither me nor my Father. If you had known me, you would have known the Father also.

"I am going away, and you will look for me, but you will die in your sin. Where I am going, you cannot come. You are from beneath and I am from above; you are of this world, I am not of this world. This is why I say to you that you shall die in your sins: if you do not believe that I am He, you will die in your sins."

Jesus, when the people then asked Him who He really was, said, "Just what I have been telling you from the beginning! I have a great deal to say and to condemn concerning you; but the one who sent me is true, and I declare to the world those things I have heard from Him.

"When you have lifted up the Son of Man, then you will realize that I am He, and that I do nothing on my own, but I speak these things as the Father has instructed me. And the One Who sent me is with me; He has not left me alone, for I always do what is pleasing to Him."

36   The assertion of "I Am"

Jesus, when some accused Him of being a Gentile and having a demon, said, "I have no demon; rather, I honor my Father, and you dishonor me. Yet I do not seek my own glory; there is One who seeks and is the judge.

Believe me when I tell you that whoever keeps my word will never see death."

Jesus, when His listeners answered that Abraham and the prophets died and asked if He were greater, said, "If I glorify myself, my glory is nothing. It is my Father who glorifies me, He of whom you say, 'He is our God,' though you do not know Him. But I know Him. If I were to say that I do not know Him, I would be a liar like you. But I do know Him and I keep His word. Your ancestor Abraham rejoiced that he would see my day; he saw it and was glad."

Jesus, when the people jeered by saying, "You are not yet fifty years old, and have you seen Abraham?" said, "Before Abraham was, I am."

37   His role as self-sacrificing shepherd and doorway

Jesus said, "Truly I tell you, anyone who does not enter the sheepfold by the door but climbs over by some other way is a thief and a robber. But the one who enters through the door is the shepherd of the sheep. The doorkeeper opens the door for him, and the sheep hear his voice. He calls his own sheep by name and leads them out. When he brings out all his own, he goes ahead of them, and the sheep follow him because they know his voice. They will not follow a stranger but will run from him because they do not know the voice of strangers.

"Most earnestly I tell you, I am the door for the sheep. All who came before me are thieves and robbers; but the sheep did not listen to them. I am the door. Whoever enters by me will be saved, and will come in and go out and find pasture. The thief comes only to steal and kill and destroy. I have come that they may have life, and have it abundantly.

"I am the good shepherd. The good shepherd lays down his life for the sheep. But one who is a hired hand and not the shepherd and who does not own the sheep sees the wolf coming and leaves the sheep and runs away; and the wolf snatches them and scatters them. The hired hand flees because he is a hired hand and cares not at all for the sheep. I am the good shepherd and know my sheep and am known by them. Just as the Father knows me, so I know the Father. And I lay down my life for the sheep.

"I have other sheep that are not of this fold. I must bring them also, and they will listen to my voice; and there will be one flock, one shepherd. For this reason the Father loves me, because I lay down my life in order that I might take it up again. No one takes it from me, but I lay it down of my own accord. I have power to lay it down, and I have power to take it up again. This command I have received from my Father."

38   The importance to Heaven of every repentant convert

Jesus said, "The Son of Man has come to save that which was lost. Now what do you think? If a shepherd has a hundred sheep and one of them has gone astray, does he not leave the ninety-nine on the mountains and go in search of the one that went astray until he finds it? And once he has found it, he lays it across his shoulders and, I tell you, he rejoices over it more than over the ninety-nine that never went astray. And when he gets home, he calls all of his friends and neighbors together and says to them, 'Come, rejoice with me, because I have found my sheep that was lost.'

"Just so, it is not the will of your Father in heaven that one of these little ones should be lost; and there will be more joy in heaven over one sinner who repents than over ninety-nine righteous folk who need no repentance.

"Or what woman who has ten silver coins, if she loses one of them, does not light the lamp, sweep the house, and search diligently until she finds it? Then, once she has found it, she calls together her friends and neighbors, saying, 'Rejoice with me, for I have found the coin that I had lost.'

"Just so, I tell you, there is joy in the presence of the angels of God over one sinner who repents."

39   Second summary of the Law and the Tradition

Jesus, having been asked by one of the scribes which was the first and greatest of the commandments, said, "The first is, 'Hear, O Israel: the Lord our God, the Lord is one; you shall love the Lord your God with all your heart, and with all your soul, and with all your mind, and with all your strength.' This is the first and greatest commandment, and a second is like unto it.

"The second is this, 'You shall love your neighbor as yourself.' There is no other commandment greater than these. On these two hang all the law and the prophets."

Jesus, when the scribe agreed with Him before the people, said, "You are not far from the Kingdom of God."

40   The salvific role of the Law

Jesus, upon being asked by a lawyer in the crowd what he must do to gain eternal life, said, "What is written in the law? How do you read it?"

Jesus, as soon as the lawyer had answered, "You shall love the Lord your God with all your heart and with all your soul and with all your strength and with all your mind; and your neighbor as yourself," said, "You have answered right. Do this, and you will live."

41   The parable of the good Gentile

Jesus, having been asked by a lawyer to define who one's "neighbor" is, said, "A certain man went down from Jerusalem to Jericho, and fell into the hands of robbers, who stripped him of his clothes, beat him, and then went away, leaving him half dead. Now by chance a priest came down that same road; and when he saw the wounded man, he passed by on the other side. Likewise a Levite, when he came to the place where the man was and saw him, passed by on the other side. But a Samaritan, while he was traveling that road, came near the victim; and when he saw him, he was moved with pity. He went to him and bandaged his wounds, pouring oil and wine on them. Then he put the wounded man on his own animal, brought him to an inn, and took care of him. On the following day, the Samaritan took out two denarii, gave them to the innkeeper, and said, 'Take care of him; and whatever more you spend, when I come back, I will repay you.'

"Now, which of these three men, do you think, was a neighbor to the one who fell into the hands of the robbers?"

Jesus, when his interrogator answered, "The one who showed him mercy," said, "Go and do likewise."

42   On forgiveness

Jesus said, "Whenever you stand praying, forgive anything you have held against another; so that your Father who is in heaven may also forgive you your trespasses."

43   On persistence in prayer

Jesus said, "Which of you has a friend and shall go to him at midnight and say to him, 'Friend, lend me three loaves of bread; for a friend of mine has arrived, and I have nothing to set before him'; and the householder will answer from within, 'Do not bother me; the door has already been locked, and my children are with me in bed; I cannot get up and give you anything'?

"But I tell you, even though the second householder will not get up and give the man anything because he is his friend, yet because of his persistence the landlord will get up and give him as much as he needs."

44   On the relative importance of blood ties

Jesus, when a woman in the crowd cried out, "Blessed is the womb that bore you and the breasts that suckled you!" turned to her and said, "Rather, blessed are those who hear the word of God and keep it."

45   Concerning those who are clergy and professional functionaries of established religion

Jesus, speaking to the crowds and to His disciples, said, "The scribes and the Pharisees sit on Moses' seat. Whatever they teach you, follow it; but do not do as they do, for they do not practice what they teach. They tie up heavy burdens, hard to bear, and lay them on the shoulders of others; but they themselves are unwilling to lift a finger to move them. They do all their deeds to be seen by others; for they make their phylacteries broad and their fringes long. They love to have the place of honor at banquets and the best seats in the synagogues, and to be greeted with respect in the marketplaces, and to have people call them rabbi.

"But you are not to be called rabbi, for you have one teacher, and you are all students. And call no one your father on earth, for you have one Father—the one in heaven. Nor are you to be called instructors, for you have one instructor, the Messiah. The greatest among you will be your servant. All who exalt themselves will be humbled, and all who humble themselves will be exalted.

"But woe to you, scribes and Pharisees, hypocrites! For you lock people out of the kingdom of heaven. For you do not go in yourselves, and when others are going in, you stop them.

"Woe to you, scribes and Pharisees, hypocrites! For you cross sea and land to make a single convert, and you make the new convert twice as much a child of hell as yourselves.

"Woe to you, blind guides, who say, 'Whoever swears by the sanctuary is bound by nothing, but whoever swears by the gold of the sanctuary is bound by the oath.' You blind and foolish men! Which is greater, the gold or the holy place that has made the gold sacred? And you say, 'Whoever swears by the altar is bound by nothing, but whoever swears by the gift that is on the altar is bound by the oath.' How blind you are! For which is greater, the gift or the altar that makes the gift sacred? Whoever swears by the altar swears by it and by everything on it; and whoever swears by the sanctuary swears by it and by the one who dwells in it; and whoever swears by heaven swears by the throne of God and by the one who is seated upon it.

"Woe to you, scribes and Pharisees, hypocrites! For you tithe mint and rue, dill and cumin and all manner of herbs, yet you have neglected the weightier matters of the law: justice and mercy, faith and the love of God. It is these you ought to have practiced without neglecting the others. You blind guides! You strain out a gnat but swallow a camel!

"Woe to you, scribes and Pharisees, blind hypocrites! For you clean the outside of the cup and of the plate, but inside they are full of greed and self-indulgence. O foolish Pharisee! First clean the inside of the cup, so that the outside also may become clean.

"Woe to you, scribes and Pharisees, blind hypocrites! For you are like whitewashed tombs, which on the outside look beautiful but inside are full of the bones of the dead and of all kinds of filth. So you also on the outside look righteous to others, but inside you are full of hypocrisy and lawlessness."

Jesus, when He was interrupted by a lawyer, said, "Woe to you lawyers also! For you too load people down with burdens hard to bear and then do not yourselves touch those burdens with so much as a finger."

Jesus, returning to His prior teaching, said, "Woe to you, scribes and Pharisees, blind hypocrites! For you build the tombs of the prophets and decorate the graves of the righteous, and you say, 'If we had lived in the days of our ancestors, we would not have taken part with them in shedding the blood of the prophets.' Thus you testify against yourselves that you are descendants of those who murdered the prophets. Fill up, then, the measure of your ancestors.

"You snakes, you brood of vipers! How can you escape being sentenced to hell?

"Therefore the Wisdom of God said, 'I will send you prophets and sages, apostles and scribes, some of whom you will kill and crucify, and some you will flog in your synagogues and pursue from town to town, so that upon you may come all the righteous blood shed on earth, from the blood of righteous Abel to the blood of Zechariah, son of Barachiah, whom you murdered between the sanctuary and the altar. Truly I tell you, all this will come upon this generation.

"And yes, woe to you lawyers! For you have taken away the key of knowledge; you did not enter yourselves, and you hindered those who were entering."

46 Concerning discernment instead of signs

Jesus said, "When it is evening, you say, 'It will be fine weather tomorrow, because the sky is red.' And in the morning, you say, 'It will storm today, because the sky is red and threatening.' You see a cloud rising in the west, and immediately you say, 'It is going to rain,' and so it happens. And when you perceive the south wind blowing, you say, 'There will be scorching heat,' and it happens. You hypocrites! You know how to interpret the appearance of earth and sky, why do you not know how to interpret the present time?

"A wicked and adulterous generation seeks after signs, and no sign shall be given it, except the sign of the prophet Jonah."

47   Human vulnerability and the call to repentance

Jesus, when asked by the crowd if some Galileans whom Pilate had slaughtered were worse sinners than all other Galileans, said, "Do you think that these Galileans were worse sinners than all other Galileans because they suffered such things? No, but I tell you: unless you repent, you will all likewise perish. Or those eighteen who were killed when the tower of Siloam fell on them—do you think that they were worse offenders than all the others living in Jerusalem? No, but I tell you, unless you repent, you all will perish just as they did."

48   The power of petition

Jesus said, "A man had a fig tree planted in his vineyard; but when he came looking for fruit on it and found none, he said to the vinedresser, 'Look here now! For three years I have come seeking fruit on this fig tree, and still I find none. Cut it down! Why should it be using up space and wasting it?' But the vinedresser answered, 'Sir, let it alone this year, until I can dig around it and put manure on it. If it bears fruit next year, well and good; but if not, then you can cut it down.'"

49   The testimony of His objective acts

Jesus, when the crowd took up stones to stone Him, said, "I have shown you many good works from the Father. For which of these are you going to stone me?"

Jesus, when they answered that it was because He was claiming to be God that were going to stone Him, said, "Is it not written in your law, 'I said, "You are gods"'? If He called those to whom the word of God came 'gods'—and the scripture cannot be denied—how is it you can say that the one whom the Father has sanctified and sent into the world is blaspheming because I said, 'I am God's Son'? If I am not doing the works of my Father, then do not believe me. But if I do them, even though you do not believe me, believe the works, so that you may know and believe that the Father is in me and I am in the Father."

50   The end of Time

Jesus said, "When, once the Master of the house has gotten up and shut the door, and you begin to stand outside knocking at the door and saying, 'Lord, open to us,' then he will answer and say to you, 'I do not know you or where you come from.' Then you will begin to say, 'We ate and drank in your presence, and you taught in our streets.' But he will say, 'I tell you, I do not know where you come from. Depart from me, all you evildoers!'

"There will be weeping and gnashing of teeth when you see Abraham and Isaac and Jacob and all the prophets inside the Kingdom of God, and you yourselves are cast out. I tell you, many will come from east and west, from north and south, and will sit at table with Abraham, Isaac, and Jacob in the Kingdom of God, while the sons of the kingdom will be exiled into the outer darkness where men and women will weep and gnash their teeth. Indeed, many who are first will be last, and the last will be first."

51   Prophecy of the Triumphal Entry

Jesus said, "O, Jerusalem, Jerusalem, killing the prophets and stoning those who are sent to you! How often would I have gathered your children together as a hen gathers her brood under her wings, and you would not! See, your house is desolate and forsaken. And I tell you, you will not see me again until the time comes when you say, 'Blessed is the one who comes in the name of the Lord.'"

52   The place of government in the believer's life

Jesus, when the Pharisees tried to trick Him by asking whether or not it was legal to pay taxes to Caesar, said, "Why do you put me to the test, you hypocrites? Bring me the coin for paying the tax and let me look at it."

Jesus, when they had brought Him a tax token, said, "Whose image and inscription are these?"

Jesus, when they told Him Caesar's, said, "Why then, render to Caesar the things that are Caesar's and to God the things that are God's."

53   The cost of choosing to join the Kingdom

Jesus said, "Who among you, if he is intending to build a tower, does not first sit down and estimate the cost, to see whether he has enough resources to complete it? If he did not do so, when he has laid a foundation and is not able to finish, everyone who sees it will begin to laugh at him, 'Look here. This poor fellow began to build but was not able to finish.' Or what king, going out to make war against another king, does not sit down first and consider whether he is able with ten thousand soldiers to oppose the one who comes against him with twenty thousand? If he cannot, then, while the other is still a great way off, he sends a delegation and asks for the terms of peace. So likewise, whoever of you does not give up all his or her possessions cannot be my disciple."

54   The parable of the prodigal son

Jesus said, "There was a man who had two sons. The younger of them said to his father, 'Father, give me the portion of goods that will belong to me.' So he divided his property between them. Not many days later the younger son gathered all he had, journeyed to a far country, and there squandered his wealth in dissolute living. But when he had spent everything, there came a severe famine in that country, and he began to be in need. So he went and hired himself out to one of the citizens of that country, who sent him into his fields to feed the pigs. He would gladly have filled his belly with the pods that the pigs were eating; and no one gave him anything.

"But when he came to himself he said, 'How many of my father's hired servants have bread enough and to spare, but I am perishing of hunger! I will get up and go to my father, and I will say to him, "Father, I have sinned against heaven and before you; I am no longer worthy to be called your son; treat me like one of your hired servants."' So he arose and went to his father.

"But while he was still a great way off, his father saw him and had compassion and ran and put his arms around him and kissed him. Then the son said to him, 'Father, I have sinned against heaven and before you; I am no longer worthy to be called your son.' But the father said to his servants, 'Bring out the best robe and put it on him; and put a ring on his finger and sandals on his feet. And bring the fatted calf and kill it, and let us eat and be merry; for this son of mine was dead and is alive again; he was lost and is found!' And they began to celebrate.

"Now, the elder son was in the field; and as he came and approached the house, he heard music and dancing. He called one of the servants and asked what these things meant. The servant replied, 'Your brother has come, and your father has killed the fatted calf, because he received him back safe and sound.' Then he became angry and would not go in. So, his father came out and began to plead with him. But he answered his father, 'Lo, these many years I have been serving you, and I have never disobeyed your command; yet you have never given me a young goat that I might make merry with my friends. But as soon as this son of yours came back, who has devoured your property with prostitutes, you killed the fatted calf for him!' Then the father said to him, 'Son, you

are always with me, and all that I have is yours. But it is
right that we should celebrate and rejoice, for this your
brother was dead and is alive again, was lost and now is
found.'"

55   The story of the rich man in Hell

Jesus said, "There was a certain rich man who was dressed
in purple and fine linen and who feasted sumptuously
every day. And there was a beggar named Lazarus, covered
with sores, who was laid at his gate, longing to be fed
with whatever crumbs fell from the rich man's table;
moreover, the dogs came and licked his sores. So it
happened that the beggar died and was carried away by
the angels to Abraham's bosom. The rich man also died
and was buried. And in Hades, where he was in torment,
he looked up and saw Abraham afar off and with Lazarus
by his side. He cried out, 'Father Abraham, have mercy on
me, and send Lazarus to dip the tip of his finger in water
and cool my tongue; for I am tormented in these flames.'
But Abraham said, 'Son, remember that in your lifetime
you received your good things, and Lazarus evil things;
but now he is comforted, and you are in agony. Besides
all this, between you and us there is a great gulf fixed, so
that those who want to pass from here to you cannot, nor
can those from there pass to us.' He said, 'Then, father,
I beg you to send him to my father's house—for I have
five brothers—that he may warn them, lest they also
come into this place of torment.' Abraham replied, 'They
have Moses and the prophets; let them hear them.' He
said, 'No, father Abraham; but if someone goes to them
from the dead, they will repent.' But he said to him, 'If

they do not listen to Moses and the prophets, neither will they be persuaded even if someone were to rise from the dead.'"

56   The assertion of Now

Jesus said, "The Kingdom of God is not coming with things that can be observed; nor will they say, 'See, here it is!' or 'Look, there it is!' For, behold, the Kingdom of God is in the midst of you."

57   The definition of prayer that is heard and received

Jesus said, "Two men went up to the Temple to pray, one a Pharisee and the other a tax collector. The Pharisee stood and prayed thus with himself: 'God, I thank you that I am not like other people: thieves, rogues, adulterers, or even like this tax collector. I fast twice a week; I give a tithe of all I have.' But the tax collector, standing far off, would not even so much as raise his eyes up to heaven, but was beating his breast and saying, 'God, be merciful to me, a sinner!' I tell you, this man went down to his home justified rather than the other."

58   On marriage, divorce, and celibacy

Jesus, having been asked by the Pharisees whether it was lawful to divorce one's wife for any cause, said, "What did Moses command you? Have you not read that from the beginning of creation itself, the one who made them 'made them male and female'? For this reason a man shall leave his father and mother and be joined to his wife, and the two shall become one flesh. So they are no longer two but one flesh. What, therefore, God has joined together, let no one pull asunder."

Jesus, when they asked Him why Moses had then allowed divorce, said, "It was because you were so hardhearted that Moses allowed you to set aside your wives and give them writs of divorce, but from the beginning it was not so. And I say to you, whoever divorces his wife, except for reasons of sexual immorality, causes her to commit adultery. And whoever marries a woman divorced from her husband commits adultery. And whoever, having divorced his wife, marries another commits adultery against her. And if a woman divorces her husband and marries someone else, she commits adultery."

Jesus, when asked by His disciples if it were not better then not to marry, said, "Not everyone can accept this teaching, but only those to whom it is given. For there are eunuchs who have been so from birth, and there are eunuchs who have been made eunuchs by others, and there are eunuchs who have made themselves eunuchs for the sake of the kingdom of heaven. Let anyone accept this who can."

59   The cleansing of the Temple

Jesus, as He was driving the money changers out of the Temple, said, "Take all this out of here! Do not make my Father's house a place of goods and merchandise! It is written: 'My house shall be called a house of prayer'; but you have made it a den of thieves."

60   The prophecy of the Resurrection

Jesus, when asked by the crowds what sign He might show them, said, "Destroy this Temple, and in three days I will raise it up."

61   A reprimand to the established clergy

Jesus, when the priests and scribes became angry that the crowds were glorifying Him, turned to them and said, "Have you never read what is written: 'Out of the mouths of infants and nursing children you have perfected praise'?"

62   Exposing the weakness of arguing from doctrine

Jesus, when asked by the Pharisees to state the authority by which He taught, said, "I will also ask you a question. Tell me now, the baptism of John, was it from heaven or from men? Answer me."

   Jesus, when the Pharisees were unable to answer Him, said, "Then neither will I tell you by what authority I do these things."

63   Condemnation of the socially righteous

Jesus said, "What do you think? A man had two sons; he went to the first and said, 'Son, go work in the vineyard today.' He answered and said, 'I will not'; but later he repented and went. The father went to the second and said the same thing; and he answered, 'I go, sir'; but he did not go. Which of the two did the will of his father?"

Jesus, when they answered "The first," turned to them and said, "Truly I tell you, that the tax collectors and the prostitutes are going into the Kingdom of God ahead of you. For John came to you in the way of righteousness and you did not believe him, but the tax collectors and the prostitutes believed him; and you, even after you had seen it, did not repent so that you might believe in him."

64 His role as "the stone rejected by the builders"

Jesus said, "Listen to another parable. There was a certain landowner who planted a vineyard, put a fence around it, dug a place for the wine vat, and built a watchtower. Then he leased it out to tenants and went to another country. When the harvest time had come, he sent his servants to the tenants to collect his produce. But the tenants seized the servants and beat one, and killed another, and stoned another. Then he sent other slaves, more than the first; and they treated them in the same way. Having yet one son, his beloved, he last of all sent the young man to them, saying, 'They will respect my son.' But when the tenants saw the son, they said to themselves, 'This is the heir; come, let us kill him and steal his inheritance.' So they seized him, threw him out of the vineyard, and killed him. Now, when the owner of the vineyard comes, what will he do to those tenants?"

Jesus, when the people answered Him that the owner will kill the tenants and give the vineyard's care over to new tenants, said, "Yes, he will come and destroy the tenants and give the vineyard to others. What is it then that is written? Have you never read in the scriptures, 'The stone that the builders rejected has become the cornerstone; this is the Lord's doing, and it is marvelous in our eyes'?

"Therefore I tell you, the Kingdom of God will be taken away from you and given to a people that produces the fruits of the kingdom. And whoever shall fall on this stone will be broken to pieces; and it will crush anyone on whom it falls."

65   The eternal life of the worthy

Jesus, when asked by the Sadducees, who did not believe in the resurrection, about marriage in the after-life, said, "Is not this the reason you are wrong, because you do not know either the scriptures or the power of God? The children of this age marry and are given in marriage; but those who are found worthy to attain that age and to the resurrection from the dead neither marry nor are given in marriage, for they cannot die anymore but are like angels in heaven and are children of God, being children of the resurrection. And as for the dead being raised, have you not read in the book of Moses what was said to you by God in the story about the bush, how God said, 'I am the God of Abraham, the God of Isaac, and the God of Jacob'? He is not God of the dead, but of the living; you are quite wrong."

66   The great paradox

Jesus, speaking to the crowd, said, "What do you think of the Christ? Whose son is he?"

Jesus, when the crowd answered that the Christ was David's son, said, "How is it that the scribes can say that the Messiah is the son of David? David himself, inspired by the Holy Spirit, said, 'The Lord said to my Lord, "Sit at my right hand, until I put your enemies under your feet."' If David himself thus calls him 'Lord,' how can he be his son?"

BOOK II

The Words of Private Instruction

1 Heaven and earth, spirit and flesh

Jesus, when He was sought out by a leader of the people under cover of darkness for instruction, said, "Truly, no one can see the Kingdom of God without being born from above. Indeed and in truth, I tell you, no one can enter the Kingdom of God without being born of water and Spirit. What is born of the flesh is flesh, and what is born of the Spirit is spirit. Do not be astonished that I said to you, 'You must be born from above.' The wind blows where it chooses, and you hear the sound of it, but you do not know where it comes from or where it goes. So it is with everyone who is born of the Spirit."

Jesus, when asked by His visitor how this could be, said, "Are you a teacher of Israel, and yet you do not understand these things? Believe me when I tell you that we speak of what we know and testify to what we have seen; yet you do not receive our testimony. If I have told you about earthly things and you do not believe, how can you believe if I tell you about heavenly things? No one has ascended into heaven except the one who descended from heaven, the Son of Man. And just as Moses lifted up the serpent in the wilderness, so must the Son of Man be lifted up in order that whoever believes in him may have eternal life. For God so loved the world that He gave His only Son, so that everyone who believes in him may not perish but may have eternal life.

"Indeed, God did not send the Son into the world to condemn the world, but in order that the world might be saved through him. Those who believe in him are not condemned; but those who do not believe are condemned already, because they have not believed in the name of the only Son of God. And this is the judgment, that the light has come into the world, and people loved darkness rather than light because their deeds were evil. For all who do evil hate the light and do not come to the light, lest their deeds be exposed. But those who do what is true come to the light, so that it may be clearly seen that their deeds have been done in God."

2   The assertion of His messiahship and of a new way of worship

Jesus, resting on His journey to Samaria at a well near Sychar, saw a woman drawing water there and said, "Give me something to drink."

Jesus, when the woman questioned Him about why a Jew would ask water of a Samaritan, said, "If you knew the gift of God and who it is that says to you, 'Give me a drink,' you would have asked him to give you living water, and he would have."

Jesus, when asked by her if He were a greater man than Jacob who first dug the well, said, "Everyone who drinks of this water will be thirsty again, but those who drink of the water that I will give them will never be thirsty. The water that I will give will become in them a spring of water gushing up to eternal life. As the scripture has said of anyone who believes in me, 'Out of his heart shall flow rivers of living water.'"

Jesus, when the woman asked Him for such water, said, "Go call your husband and come back."

Jesus, when she told Him she had no husband, said, "You are right in saying, 'I have no husband'; for you have had five husbands, and the one you have now is not your husband. What you have said is true!"

Jesus, when the woman declared that He was indeed a prophet, said, "Woman, believe me, the hour is coming when you will worship the Father neither on this mountain nor in Jerusalem. You worship what you do not know; we worship what we know, for salvation is from the Jews. But the hour is coming, and is now here, when the true worshipers will worship the Father in spirit and truth, for the Father seeks such as these to worship Him. God is spirit, and those who worship Him must worship in spirit and truth."

Jesus, when the woman told Him that she knew the Messiah was to come, said, "I who speak to you am he."

3   An admonition about greed

Jesus, when asked by a man in the crowd to tell his brother
to divide an inheritance with him, said, "Man, who made
me a judge or an arbiter over you? Take heed, rather, and
beware of greediness, for a person's life does not consist
in the abundance of things he or she may possess."

4   The utter primacy of devotion over any other necessities

Jesus, speaking to a scribe who wished to follow Him,
said, "Foxes have holes, and birds of the air have nests,
but the Son of Man has nowhere to lay his head."

Jesus said to another in the crowd, "Follow me."

Jesus, when the man asked for time first to bury his
father, then said to him, "Let the dead bury their own
dead; but as for you, go and proclaim the Kingdom of
God."

Jesus, to a third man who wished to follow Him
later, said, "No one who puts a hand to the plow and
looks back is fit for the Kingdom of God."

5   His description of those for whom He came

Jesus, passing by the office of Matthew, the tax collector,
said to him, "Follow me."

Jesus, sitting later at a feast in Matthew's house,
perceived that those watching wondered why He would
associate with tax collectors, and He said to them, "Those
who are well have no need of a physician, but those who
are sick. Go and learn what this means, 'I desire mercy,

not sacrifice.' For I have come to call not the righteous but sinners to repentance."

6 His assertion of the radical nature of His work

Jesus, when the disciples of John and of the Pharisees asked Him why His disciples did not fast, said to them, "The wedding guests cannot mourn nor can they fast as long as the bridegroom is with them, now, can they? The day will come when the bridegroom is taken away from them, and then they will fast at that day."

Jesus further said to them, "No one sews a piece of unshrunk cloth on an old garment; for if she does, the patch tears away from the garment—the new from the old—and a worse tear is made. Neither is new wine put into old wineskins; otherwise, the skins burst, and the wine is spilled, and the skins are destroyed; but new wine is put into fresh wineskins, and so both are preserved. New wine is for new wineskins. And no one drinking old wine desires the new, for he says, 'The old is good.'"

7 The first commissioning, of the twelve

Jesus, commissioning the twelve, said to them, "Go nowhere among the Gentiles, and enter no town of the Samaritans, but go rather to the lost sheep of the house of Israel. As you go, proclaim the good news, 'The kingdom of heaven has come near.'

"Cure the sick, raise the dead, cleanse the lepers, cast out demons. You received without payment; give without payment.

"Take nothing for your journey—no gold, or silver, or copper in your belts, no bag for your journey. Do not take sandals, or an extra tunic, or a staff, or bread; for laborers deserve their food.

"Whatever town or village you enter, find out who in it is worthy. Where you enter a house, stay there until you leave the place. As you enter the house, greet it. If the house is worthy, let your peace come upon it; but if it is not worthy, let your peace return to you. If any place receive you and if anyone will not welcome you or listen to your words, shake off the dust from your feet as you leave that house or town as a testimony against them. Truly I tell you, it will be more tolerable for the land of Sodom and Gomorrah on the day of judgment than for that town."

8   The second commissioning, of the larger company of the seventy

Jesus, commissioning seventy of His followers as emissaries of the Kingdom, said, "The harvest is plentiful, but the laborers are few; pray, therefore, asking the Lord of the harvest to send out laborers into his harvest. Go on your way. See, I am sending you out like lambs into the midst of wolves; so be as wise as serpents and as innocent as doves.

"Whatever town or village you enter, find who is worthy in it and stay with them until you depart. And whatever house you enter, first salute it, saying, 'Peace to this house!' And if the house is worthy and if a son or daughter of peace is there, your peace will rest on that person; but if not, it will return to you. Remain in the same house, eating and drinking whatever they provide, for the laborer deserves to be paid. Do not move about from house to house.

"Whenever you enter a town and its people welcome you, eat what is set before you. Heal the sick who are there, raise the dead, cleanse lepers, cast out demons. You received freely and without paying; give freely. And say to them, 'The Kingdom of God has come near to you.'

"But whenever you enter a town and they do not welcome you, go out into its streets and say, 'Even the dust of your town that clings to our feet, we wipe off in protest against you. Yet know this: the Kingdom of God has come near.' I tell you, on that day it will be more tolerable for Sodom and Gomorrah than for that town.

"Woe to you, Chorazin! Woe to you, Bethsaida! For if the mighty works done in you had been done in Tyre and Sidon, they would have repented long ago, sitting in sackcloth and ashes. But I tell you, on the judgment it will be more tolerable for Tyre and Sidon than for you. And you, Capernaum, will you be exalted to heaven? No, you will be brought down to Hades.

"Whoever listens to you listens to me, and whoever rejects you rejects me, and whoever rejects me rejects the one who sent me."

9   The first graphic and detailed discussion of the interplay between good and evil

Jesus, when the seventy emissaries returned to Him with joy in their work, said, "I saw Satan fall from heaven like a flash of lightning. See, I have given you authority to tread on snakes and scorpions, and over all the power of the enemy; and nothing will hurt you. Nevertheless, do not rejoice at this, that the spirits submit to you, but rejoice that your names are written in heaven."

Jesus, at that same moment, rejoiced in the Spirit and said, "I thank You, Father, Lord of heaven and earth, because You have hidden these things from the wise and the intelligent and have revealed them to infants; yes, Father, for such was Your gracious will. All things have been delivered over to me by my Father; and no one knows who the Son is except the Father, or who the Father is except the Son, and anyone to whom the Son chooses to reveal Him."

Jesus then, turning to the disciples, privately said, "Blessed are the eyes that see what you see! For I tell you that many prophets and kings desired to see what you see, but did not see it, and to hear what you hear, but did not hear it."

10   The prophecies of persecutions to come and of their proper endurance

Jesus, counseling His disciples, said, "As for yourselves, beware of people; for they will hand you over to councils and flog you in their synagogues; and you will be dragged before governors and kings because of me. This will be the time for you to bear testimony to them and to the Gentiles. And the good news must first be proclaimed to all nations.

"Settle it then in your minds: When they bring you to trial and deliver you up, do not be anxious about how you are to speak and do not worry beforehand about what you are to say; for what you are to say will be given you in that hour and at that time. It is not you who speak, but the Holy Spirit, the Spirit of your Father speaking through you.

"Brother will betray brother to death, and a father his child, and children will rise against parents and have them put to death; and you will be hated by all because of my name. But the one who endures to the end will be saved.

"When they persecute you in one town, flee to the next; for truly I tell you, you will not have gone through all the towns of Israel before the Son of Man comes.

"Can a blind person guide a blind person? Will they not both fall into a hole? A disciple is not above the teacher, nor is a servant above the master. But everyone who is fully taught will be like the master and informed like the teacher; and this is enough.

"If they have called the master of the house Beelzebul, how much more will they malign those of his household? So have no fear of them; for nothing is covered up that will not be uncovered, and nothing hidden that will not become known. Whatever you have said in the dark shall be heard in the light, and what you have whispered in private rooms shall be shouted from the rooftops. What I say to you in the dark, tell in the light; and what you hear whispered, proclaim from the housetops.

"My friends, do not fear those who kill the body and, after that, have no more that they can do for they cannot kill the soul. I will tell you whom to fear: fear Him who, after He has killed, has power to cast into hell, to destroy both soul and body in hell. Yes, I tell you, fear that One!

"Are not two sparrows sold for a penny or five for two coppers? Yet not one of them will fall to the ground apart from your Father. And even the hairs of your head are all counted. So do not be afraid; you are of more value than many sparrows.

"Everyone, therefore, who acknowledges me before other people, I also will acknowledge before my Father in heaven and before the angels of God; but whoever in this adulterous and sinful generation is ashamed of me and denies me before others, the Son of Man will also be ashamed of when he comes in the glory of his Father and I will deny before my Father in heaven and before the angels of God."

11   The cost of membership in His Kingdom

Jesus, speaking to the twelve, said, "Anyone who loves father or mother more than me is not worthy of me. Anyone who comes to me and does not hate father and mother, wife and children, brothers and sisters, and yes, even life itself, cannot be my disciple. And whoever does not take up and carry his or her own cross and follow after me is not worthy of me and cannot be my disciple. Anyone who seeks to find his or her life will lose it; and anyone who loses life for my sake and the gospel's will find and preserve it."

12   The rewards of honoring His Kingdom and its citizens

Jesus, speaking to His disciples, said, "Whoever welcomes you whom I have sent welcomes me; and anyone who welcomes me welcomes and receives the One who sent me. Any person who welcomes a prophet in the name of a prophet will receive a prophet's reward; and anybody who welcomes a righteous person in the name of a righteous person will receive the reward of the righteous; and anyone who gives even a cup of cold water to one of these little ones because he is a disciple— truly I tell you, that person will not lose his or her reward."

13   The direct bestowal of personal salvation

Jesus, while eating in the house of a Pharisee, was approached by a woman who began to bathe His feet in ointment; and He, turning to His host, said, "Simon, I have something to say to you: A certain creditor had two debtors; one owed five hundred denarii, and the other fifty. When neither could pay, he canceled the debts for both of them. Now which of these two will love him more?"

Jesus, when Simon answered, "I suppose the one for whom he canceled the greater debt," said, "You have judged rightly. Now do you see this woman? I entered your house; you gave me no water for my feet, but she has bathed my feet with her tears and dried them with her hair. You gave me no kiss, but from the time I came in she has not stopped kissing my feet. You did not anoint my head with oil, but she has anointed my feet with ointment. Therefore, I tell you, her sins, which were many, have been forgiven; hence she has shown great love. But the one to whom little is forgiven, loves little."

Jesus, speaking to the woman, said, "Your sins are forgiven. Your faith has saved you; go in peace."

14   Mercy as the mediator of all religious law

Jesus, when His disciples were accused of breaking Sabbath law by eating grain from the fields in which they
were walking, turned to their accusers and said, "Have
you never read what David did when he was hungry,
he and those with him? He entered the house of God,
when Abiathar was high priest, and ate the bread of the
Presence, which it was not lawful for him to eat, but only
for the priests. And he gave it to his companions as well.

"Or have you not read in the law that on the Sabbath
the priests in the Temple break the Sabbath and yet are
guiltless? I tell you, something greater than the Temple
is here. But if you had known what this means, 'I desire
mercy and not sacrifice,' you would not have condemned
the guiltless. For the Son of Man is Lord of the Sabbath."

15   On how understanding increases
with understanding

Jesus, to a group of followers gathered around Him, said,
"To you it has been given to know the secrets of the
kingdom of heaven, but to the crowds it has not been
given. For to those who have, more will be given, and
they will have an abundance; but from those who have
nothing, even what they have will be taken away.

"The reason I speak in parables to those outside is
that 'seeing, they do not perceive, and hearing, they do
not listen, nor do they understand.' With them indeed is
fulfilled the prophecy of Isaiah that says:

'You will indeed listen, but never understand,
and you will indeed look, but never perceive.

For this people's heart has grown dull,
and their ears are hard of hearing,
and they have shut their eyes;
so that they might not look with their eyes,
and listen with their ears,
and understand with their heart and turn—
and I would heal them.'"

16   Private exegesis on the parable of the sower

Jesus, when questioned by His disciples about the parable of the sower, said "Do you not understand this parable? How then will you understand any of the parables? Hear then the parable of the sower.

"The seed is the word of God. When anyone hears the word of the kingdom and does not understand it, the devil comes and snatches away the word from his or her heart, lest they believe and be saved; this is what was sown on the path. And as for that which was sown on rocky ground, that is one who hears the word and immediately receives it with joy; yet he or she, having no root, believes and endures only for a while. And when temptation comes or when trouble and persecution arise on account of the word, that person immediately falls away. As for what was sown among thorns, it is the one who hears the word, but the cares of the world and the lure of wealth and pleasure choke the word, and it yields nothing.

"But as for what was sown on good soil, this is the one who hears the word and understands it and holds it fast in an honest and faithful heart, and who indeed bears fruit and yields, in one case a hundredfold, in another sixty, and in another thirty."

17   Similes of the Kingdom

Jesus, alone with the twelve, said, "The Kingdom of God is thus: it is as if someone should plant seed on the ground, and should sleep and rise night and day, and the seed should sprout and grow, though the sower himself does not know how. The earth produces of itself, first the stalk, then the head, then the full wheat in the head. And when the grain is ripe, he immediately goes in with his sickle, because the harvest has come."

Jesus, speaking then to a group of His disciples, said, "The kingdom of heaven may be compared to a man sowing good seed in his field; but while he was asleep his enemy came and sowed tares among the wheat, and then went away. So when the wheat sprouted and came up and bore grain, then the weeds appeared as well. And the man's slaves came and said to him, 'Master, did you not sow good seed in your field? Where, then, did these weeds come from?' He answered, 'A hostile man has done this.' And the slaves said to him, 'Then do you want us to go and gather them up?' But he replied, 'No, lest in gathering the tares you uproot the wheat along with them. Leave both of them to grow together until the harvest; and at harvest time I will say to the reapers, 'Collect the weeds first and bind them in bundles to be burned, but gather the wheat into my barn.'

"With what are we able to compare the Kingdom of God, or what likeness shall we use for it? The kingdom of heaven is like a mustard seed that someone took and sowed in his garden.

"It is the smallest of all the seeds on earth, but yet, when it has grown, it is the greatest of all the shrubs and becomes a tree and puts out large branches, so that the birds of the air come and make nests in its shade.

"To what shall I compare the kingdom of heaven? It is like leaven that a woman took and hid in three measures of meal until it all was leavened."

18   Exegesis on the parable of the tares

Jesus, when His disciples asked Him privately to explain the meaning of His parable of the wheat and the tares, said, "The one sowing the good seed is the Son of Man. The field is the world, and the good seeds are the children of the kingdom; the tares are the children of the evil one, and the enemy who sowed them is the devil. The harvest is the completion of the age, and the reapers are angels.

"Just as the weeds, therefore, are collected and burned up with fire, so will it be at the end of this age. The Son of Man will send his angels, and they will collect out of his kingdom all the offensive things and all who are doing evil; and they will throw them into the furnace of fire, where there will be weeping and gnashing of teeth. Then the righteous will shine like the sun in the kingdom of their Father. Let anyone having ears to hear, listen!"

19   Continuation of similes for comprehending the Kingdom

Jesus, teaching His disciples, said, "The kingdom of heaven is like treasure that, having been hidden in a field, someone finds, hides again, and then in joy goes and sells all that he has and buys that field.

"Again, the kingdom of heaven is like a merchant in search of beautiful pearls who, on finding a very valuable one, went out and sold all that he had and bought it.

"Again, the kingdom of heaven is like a dragnet that was thrown into the sea and caught fish of every kind. When it was full, the fishermen drew it ashore, sat down, and put the good fish into baskets but threw out the rotten ones.

"So it will be at the end of the age. The angels will come out and separate the evil people from out of the midst of the righteous and will throw them into the furnace of fire, where there will be weeping and gnashing of teeth. Have you understood all this?"

Jesus, as soon as the disciples told Him that they had understood, said, "On account of this, every scribe who has been trained for the kingdom of heaven is like the master of a household who brings out of his treasure both what is new and what is old."

20   The offense, for His disciples, of the teachings about the Kingdom

Jesus, when His disciples were disturbed by His teaching, said, "Does this offend you? Then what if you shall see the Son of Man ascending to where he was before? It is the spirit that gives life; the flesh profits nothing. The words that I have spoken to you, they are spirit and they are life. But there are some among you that believe not. For this reason I have told you that no one can come to me unless it is granted by the Father."

Jesus, when many who were following Him turned away, challenged the twelve and said, "Do you also wish to turn away?"

Jesus, when Peter answered that they knew Him to be the Son of God, said, "Did I not choose you twelve? Yet one of you is a devil."

21   The offense, for orthodox Jewish leaders, of the teachings about the Kingdom

Jesus, when told by His disciples that the Pharisees were offended by his kingdom teachings, said, "Every plant that my Father has not planted will be rooted up. Let them alone. They are blind guides; and if a blind man leads a blind man, they will both fall into a pit."

22   Exegesis on the defilement teachings

Jesus, when asked by His disciples about the meaning of His teaching on defilement, said, "Then do you also fail to understand? Listen to me. Do you not see that whatever comes into a person from outside cannot defile him or her, for it enters, not the heart but the stomach, and goes on out into the sewer? Rather, it is what comes out of a person that defiles; for it is from within, from out of the human heart, that evil intentions come: fornication, theft, murder, adultery, avarice, wickedness, deceit, licentiousness, envy, slander, false witness, pride, folly. All these evil things come from within, and they defile a person. But to eat with unwashed hands does not defile one."

23   The danger of literalness and of religiosity

Jesus, speaking to His disciples, said, "Watch out, and beware of the yeast of the Pharisees, the Sadducees, and of Herod."

Jesus, realizing that they thought He was chastising them for having brought no food with them, said, "O you of little faith, why are you discussing among yourselves the fact that you have no bread? Do you still not perceive or understand? Are your hearts hardened? When I broke the five loaves for the five thousand, how many baskets of broken pieces did you pick up afterward? Do you not remember those five loaves for the five thousand, and how many baskets you gathered? And the seven loaves for the four thousand, how many baskets full of broken pieces did you gather? How could you fail to understand that I was not talking about bread? Beware of the leaven of the Pharisees and Sadducees, which is hypocrisy!"

24   Prophecy of the final judgment

Jesus, teaching His disciples, said, "What will it profit a person to gain the whole world but forfeit or lose their life? Or what will a person give in return for his life? For whoever is ashamed of me and of my words in this adulterous and sinful generation, of him or her will the Son of Man also be ashamed when he comes in the glory of his Father with the holy angels. For the Son of Man is to come with his angels in the glory of his Father, and then he will repay everyone for what has been done. Truly I tell you, there are some standing here who will not taste death before they see the Son of Man coming in his kingdom with power."

25   The parable of the shrewd overseer

Jesus, speaking to His disciples, said, "There was a rich man who had an overseer, and charges were brought to him that this overseer was squandering his property. So he called the man to him and said, 'What is this that I hear about you? Give me an accounting of your work, for you cannot be my overseer any longer.'

"Then the overseer said to himself, 'What shall I do, for my master is taking my job away from me? I cannot dig, and I am ashamed to beg. But I know what to do so that, when I am dismissed as overseer, people may welcome me into their homes.' So, summoning his master's debtors one by one, he asked the first, 'How much do you owe my master?' He answered, 'A hundred measures of oil.' He said to him, 'Take your bill, sit down quickly, and make it fifty.' Then he asked another, 'And how much do you owe?' He replied, 'A hundred measures of wheat' He said to him, 'Take your bill and make it eighty.'

"So the master commended the dishonest overseer because he had acted shrewdly; for the children of this age are more shrewd in their generation than are the children of light. And I tell you, make friends for yourselves by means of dishonest wealth so that when you fail they may welcome you into an eternal home. Whoever is faithful in a very little is faithful also in much; and whoever is dishonest in a very little is dishonest also in much. If, therefore, you have not been faithful with dishonest riches, who will entrust to you the true ones? And if you have not been faithful with what belongs to another, who will give you what is your own?"

26   A prophecy of His suffering

Jesus, when they asked Him why the prophets had said that Elijah must return before all these things could be, said, "Elijah does come first to restore all these things; and how is it written of the Son of Man, that he should suffer many things and be treated with contempt? But I tell you that Elijah has come, and they did to him whatever they pleased, as it is written of him. So also the Son of Man will suffer at their hands."

27   Faith as a physical agency

Jesus, when asked by His disciples about why they could not heal a demon-possessed boy, said, "Because of your unbelief and little faith. This kind cannot be driven out by anything except prayer."

Jesus then said, "Truly I tell you that if you have faith as large as a mustard seed, you can say to this mountain, 'Move hence to over there,' and it will move. Or you could say to this sycamore tree, 'Be uprooted and replanted in the sea,' and it would do so; for nothing will be impossible to you."

28   Of the devil and true freedom from his grip

Jesus, speaking to those who had believed in Him, said, "If you continue in my word, you are truly my disciples; and you will know the truth, and the truth will make you free."

Jesus, when some of His followers were then offended by His words, said, "Very truly I tell you, anyone who commits sin is a slave to sin. The slave does not abide forever in the household, but a son abides there forever. So if the Son makes you free, you shall be free indeed. I know that you are descendants of Abraham; but yet you seek to kill me, because there is no place in you for my word. I declare what I have seen in the Father's presence; and you do what you have seen with your father.

"If you were Abraham's children, you would be doing the works of Abraham, but now you are trying to kill me, a man who has told you the truth that I heard from God. This is not what Abraham did. You do the works of your father. If God were your Father, you would love me, for I proceeded forth and came from God; nor have I come of myself, but He sent me.

"Why do you not understand what I say? Because you are not able to listen to my word. You are from your father the devil, and you want to fulfill your father's desires. He was a murderer from the beginning and does not stand in the truth, because there is no truth in him. When he lies, he speaks from out of his own nature, for he is a liar and the father of lies. But because I tell the truth, you do not believe me. Which of you convicts me of sin? If I tell the truth, why do you not believe me? Whoever is from God hears the words of God. The reason you do not hear them is that you are not from God."

29   Condemnation of those who are portals for sin

Jesus, teaching the disciples, said "It is impossible for temptations not to come, but woe to that person by whom they do come! For if any one of you put a stumbling block before one of these little ones who believe in me, it would be better if a great millstone were fastened around your neck and you were drowned in the depth of the sea. Yes, woe to the world because of stumbling blocks, but woe to the one by whom the stumbling block comes!

"For sins must come, but woe to the man by whom they come! If your hand or your foot causes you to stumble, cut it off and throw it away; it is better for you to enter life maimed or lame than to have two hands or two feet and to be thrown into the everlasting fire. And if your eye causes you to sin, tear it out and throw it away; it is better for you to enter life with one eye than to have two eyes and to be thrown into hellfire."

30 Concerning angels and their guardianship of individuals

Jesus, to His disciples, said, "Be careful that you do not look down on one who seems small or unimportant and trivial, for I say to you that in heaven their angels always behold the face of my Father Who is in heaven."

31 The process of disciplining believers

Jesus, teaching His disciples, said, "Take heed of yourselves in this: If your brother or sister sins against you, go and point out the fault when the two of you are alone. Rebuke him or her, and if he or she repents, then forgive them; for if they listen to you, you have regained them. But if you are not listened to, take along with you one or two more people so that 'by the mouth of two or three witnesses every word may be established.' If your brother or sister refuses to listen to them, tell it to the church; and if your brother or sister refuses to hear even the church, let such a one be to you as a Gentile and a tax collector. For I tell you most assuredly that whatever you bind up on earth will be bound in heaven, and whatever you set loose on earth will be loosed in heaven. Again, I say to you, if two of you agree on earth about anything you ask, it will be done for you by my Father in heaven. For where two or three are gathered in my name, I am in the midst of them."

32   On forgiveness

Jesus, when asked by Peter how many times one person should forgive another, said, "If one sins against you seven times in one day and still turns to you and says, 'I repent,' then you must forgive him or her seven times. Indeed, I do not say to you seven times, but rather seventy times seven.

"For this reason, then, the kingdom of heaven may be compared to a certain king who wanted to settle accounts with his servants. When he began the reckoning, one who owed him ten thousand talents was brought to him; and as the man could not pay, his master commanded that the man be sold, together with his wife and children and all his possessions, and that payment be made. But the slave fell down before the king, saying, 'Master, have patience with me, and I will pay you everything.' And moved with compassion, the master of that servant released him and forgave him the debt. But that same servant went out and found one of his fellow servants who owed him a hundred denarii and, seizing him by the throat, said, 'Pay me what you owe.' Then his fellow servant fell down and begged, 'Have patience with me, and I will pay you everything.' But the first servant refused; he went and threw his servant into prison until he would pay the debt.

"When their fellow servants saw what had happened, they were greatly distressed, and they went and reported to the king all that had been done. Then the lord summoned the first man and said to him, 'You wicked servant! I forgave you all that debt because you begged me. Should you not have had mercy on your fellow servant just as I had pity on you?' And the lord was angry and handed the servant over to be tortured until he would pay his entire debt.

"So too will my heavenly Father do to every one of you, if you do not forgive your brother or sister from your heart."

33   Concerning the proper attitude for anticipating His coming

Jesus, addressing His disciples, said, "Let your loins be girded for action and have your lamps lit; be like those who are waiting for the master to return from the wedding banquet, so that they may open the door to him at once, as soon as he comes and knocks. Blessed are those servants whom the master finds awake when he comes; truly I tell you, he will gird himself and have them sit down at table to eat, and he will come and serve them. If he comes during the middle of the night, or near dawn, and finds them so, blessed are those servants.

"Watch, therefore, for you do not know at what time your Lord is coming. But know this: if the owner of the house had known at what part of the night, at what hour, the thief was coming, he would have been awake and not have let his house be broken into. You, therefore, must also be ready, for the Son of Man is coming at an hour you do not expect."

Jesus, when asked by Peter if this teaching were for all or only for the disciples, said, "Who then is the faithful and wise overseer whom the master will put in charge of his slaves, to give them their allotment of food at the proper time?

"Blessed is that slave whom his master, when he comes, will find so doing. Truly I tell you, he will put that one in charge of all his possessions. But if that wicked servant says to himself, 'My master is delayed in coming,' and if he begins to beat those others, both men and women, who are his fellow servants, and if he begins to eat and drink and get drunk, the master of that servant will come on a day when the servant does not expect him and at an hour that he does not know; and the servant will be beaten with many blows and put out with the unfaithful and the hypocrites, where men and women will weep and gnash their teeth.

"Yes, the servant who knew what his master wanted but did not prepare himself or do what was wanted will receive a severe beating. But the one who did not know and so did what deserved a beating will receive a light beating. From everyone to whom much has been given, much will be required; and from the one to whom much has been entrusted, even more will be asked."

34   On the divisiveness of Kingdom membership

Jesus, speaking to the disciples, said, "I came to send fire on the earth, and how I wish it were already kindled! I have a baptism with which to be baptized, and how distressed I am until it is accomplished! Do you think that I have come to bring peace on earth? No, I have not come to bring peace, but rather a sword and division. From now in a household of five, three will be divided against two and two against three. They will be divided: father against son, and son against father; mother against daughter, and daughter against mother; mother-in-law against daughter-in-law, and daughter-in-law against mother-in-law; for one's foes will be those of one's own household."

35 Belief as a divine and protected gift

Jesus, asked by some in the Temple if He were the Messiah, said, "I have told you, and you do not believe. The works that I do in my Father's name bear witness to me; but you do not believe, because you do not belong to my sheep, as I said to you. My sheep hear my voice. I know them, and they follow me. I give them eternal life, and they will never perish; neither shall anyone snatch them out of my hand. My Father, Who has given them to me, is greater than all, and no one can snatch them out of the Father's hand. I and my Father are one."

36 About the proper approach to social class and status

Jesus, seeing how the other guests at a dinner party were vying for the best seats at the banquet table, said, "When you are invited by anyone to a wedding feast, do not sit down in the choicest seat, lest someone more distinguished than you has been invited by your host; for the one who invited both of you may come and say to you, 'Give your place to this person,' and then in shame you would begin to take the lowest place. Rather, when you are invited, go and sit down at the humblest place, so that when your host comes he may say to you, 'Friend, move up higher'; then you will be honored in the presence of all who sit at the table with you. For whoever exalts himself or herself will surely be humbled; and whoever is humble will be exalted.

"When you give a dinner or a banquet, do not invite your friends or your siblings or your kinfolk or rich neighbors, lest they invite you in return, and you would be repaid. No, when you give a banquet, invite the poor, the crippled, the lame, and the blind; and you will be blessed, because they cannot repay you. You will be repaid at the resurrection of the righteous."

37 The parable of the banquet

Jesus, responding to a comment by a fellow guest at a banquet, said, "The Kingdom of God can be compared to a king who once gave a great wedding party for his son and invited many. When the time for the dinner arrived, he sent his servant to say to those who had been invited, 'Come; for everything is ready now.' But they would not come. So he sent out other servants to say to those whom he had invited, 'Look, I have everything ready for my banquet. My oxen and fat calves are slaughtered and all is in order. Come to the marriage feast.' But each of them made light of the invitation and began to make excuses. One said, 'I have purchased a piece of land and I must go out and see it; please accept my regrets.' Another said, 'I have just bought five yoke of oxen and I am going to try them out; please accept my regrets.' A third said, 'I have just been married and so cannot come.' The rest seized the man's servants, treated them shamefully, and then killed them. When the king received word of this, he became angry and sent out his army and killed those murderers and burned their city. Then he said to his servants, 'Go quickly out into the lanes and thoroughfares of the city and invite as many as you find to the feast. Bring in the poor, the crippled, the blind, and the lame.' Then the servants said, 'Sir, what you ordered has been done, and there is still room.' Then the master said to them, 'Go out into the highways and hedgerows, and compel people to come in, so that my house may be filled. For I tell you, none of those who were invited will taste my dinner.'

"So the servants went out into the lanes and streets and gathered all whom they found, both good and bad, so that the wedding hall was filled with guests. But when the king came in to see the guests, he noticed a man there who was not wearing a wedding robe and he said to him, 'Friend, how did you get in here without a wedding robe?' And the man was speechless; but the king said to his servants, 'Bind him hand and foot, and throw him into the outer darkness, where there will be weeping and gnashing of teeth.' For many are called, but few are chosen."

38   The believer's role as indentured servant

Jesus, speaking to the disciples, said, "Which of you, having a servant who has just come in from plowing or tending sheep, will say to him 'Come at once and sit down to eat'? Would you not instead say to him, 'Prepare something for me to eat, and then put on your apron and serve me until I have eaten; after that you may eat and drink'? Do you thank the slave for doing what was commanded? I think not! So you also, when you have done all that you were commanded to do, must say, 'We are unprofitable servants; we have done only what it was our duty to do!'"

39 About His second coming and the days preceding it

Jesus, to the disciples, said, "The times are coming when you will long to see one of the days of the Son of Man, and you will not see it. For false christs and false prophets will rise up and manifest great signs and wonders in order to deceive, were such possible, even the elect. See, I have told you this beforehand. Therefore, if they say to you, 'Look there!' or 'Look here!' do not go after them, and do not follow them. If they say, 'See, he is in the wilderness,' do not go out there. If they say, 'Look, Christ is in the inner room,' do not believe it. For like the lightning that flashes from the east and lights up the sky from one side to the other, so will the Son of Man be in his day. But first he must endure much suffering and be rejected by this generation. Just as it was in the days of Noah, so will it also be in the days of the Son of Man. They ate and drank, married and were given in marriage, until the day Noah entered the ark, and the flood came and destroyed all of them. Likewise, just as it was in the days of Lot: they ate and drank, bought and sold, planted and built, but on the day that Lot left Sodom, it rained fire and sulfur from heaven and destroyed all of them. Even so will it be on the day that the Son of Man is revealed.

"On that day, let anyone who is on the housetop and has belongings in the house not come down to take them away; and likewise anyone in the field must not turn back. Remember Lot's wife. I tell you, on that night there will be two people in one bed; one will be taken and the other left. On that day there will be two men in the field; one will be taken and one left. And there will be two women grinding meal together; one will be taken and the other left."

Jesus, when asked by them where this was to be, said, "Where the corpse is, there the vultures will gather."

40   On persistence in prayer and belief in its efficacy

Jesus, in talking to the disciples, said, "There was in a certain city a judge who feared neither God nor other people. In that same city there was a widow who kept coming to him and saying, 'Grant me justice against my adversaries.' For a while he refused; but later he said to himself, 'Though I have no fear of God nor of others, yet because this widow keeps bothering me, I will grant her justice, lest she wear me out by her continually coming here.'

"Hear what the unjust judge says. And shall God not grant justice to his elect who cry to him day and night? Will he delay long in helping them? I tell you, he will quickly grant justice to them. Nevertheless, when the Son of Man comes, will he find faith on earth?"

41   The restrictive burden of temporal wealth

Jesus, having been asked, "Good Teacher, what must I do to be saved?" turned to His questioner and said, "Why do you call me good? No one is good, save God alone. You know the commandments: 'You shall not murder; You shall not commit adultery; You shall not steal; You shall not bear false witness; You shall not defraud; Honor your father and mother.' If you would enter life, keep these."

Jesus, when the man answered that he had done all these things for years, felt love for him and said, "You lack only one thing; go, sell everything you own, and give the money to the poor, and you will have treasure in heaven; then come, follow me."

Jesus, when the young man left disheartened, said to His disciples, "How hard it will be for those who have wealth to enter the Kingdom of God! Children, how hard it is to enter the Kingdom of God! I tell you that it is easier for a camel to go through the eye of a needle than for someone who is rich to enter the Kingdom of God."

Jesus, when asked who then could be saved, said, "For mortals it is impossible, but not for God; for God all things are possible."

Jesus, when Peter told Him that the disciples had left everything for Him, said, "Truly I tell you, in the age to come, when the Son of Man shall sit in glory on his throne, you who have followed me will sit on twelve thrones judging the twelve tribes of Israel. There is no one who has left house or brothers or sisters or mother or father or children or fields, for my sake and for the sake of the gospel, who will not receive a hundredfold now in this age—houses, brothers and sisters, mothers and children, and fields, with persecutions—and in the age to come eternal life.

"But you are those who have continued with me through my trials, and I bestow on you a kingdom, just as the Father has bestowed one on me, that you may eat and drink at my table and sit on thrones in my kingdom."

42   A parable of final judgments

Jesus, telling a story to His disciples, said, "The kingdom of heaven is like a landowner who went out early one morning to hire laborers for his vineyard. And when he had agreed with them for the usual daily wage, he sent them into his vineyard. He went out again about nine o'clock and saw others standing idle in the marketplace; and he said to them, 'You also go into the vineyard, and I will pay you whatever is right.' So they went. He went out again about noon and about three o'clock and did the same. And about five o'clock he went out and found still others standing around; and he said to them, 'Why are you standing here idle all day?' They said to him, 'Because no one has hired us.' He said to them, 'You also go into the vineyard.'

"When evening came, the owner of the vineyard said to his overseer, 'Call the laborers and give them their pay, beginning with the last and then going to the first.' When those hired about five o'clock came, each of them received the usual daily wage. Now, when the first came, they assumed that they would receive more; but each of them also received the usual daily wage. And when they received it, they grumbled against the landowner, saying, 'These last worked only one hour, and you have made them equal to us who have borne the burden of the day and the scorching heat.' But he replied to one of them, 'Friend, I do you no wrong. Did you not agree with me for the usual daily wage? Take what belongs to you and go; I choose to give to this last the same as I give to you. Am I not allowed to do what I choose with what belongs to me? Or are you envious because I am generous?' So the last will be first, and the first will be last."

43   About humility and self-effacement

Jesus, teaching the twelve, said, "You know that the kings of the Gentiles lord it over them and that those whom they recognize as their great ones are tyrants over them. But it is not so among you; but whoever wishes to become great among you must be your servant, and whoever wishes to be first among you must be slave of all.

"Who is greater, the one who sits at the table or the one who serves? I am among you as one who serves. For the Son of Man came not to be served but to serve, and to give his life as a ransom for many."

44   A parable about the final judgment and the time of its coming

Jesus, when His disciples began to think that His Kingdom was coming immediately, said, "A nobleman went to a distant country to receive a kingdom for himself and then to return. So he called his servants to him and entrusted his property to them; and he gave them silver pounds, each according to his ability. To one he gave ten pounds, to another five, to another two, to others one, and then said to them, 'Trade with this money until I come back.' Then he went away.

"The servant who had received ten pounds went immediately and traded with them and made ten more;

so also the one who had received five made five more; but one who had received only one pound wrapped it in a napkin and, digging a hole, buried it. The king was gone for a long while; but the citizens of his country hated him and sent a messenger after him, saying, 'We will not have this man to rule over us.'

"Then it came to pass that when he returned, having received the kingdom, he summoned the servants to whom he had given the money so that he might find out what each of them had gained by trading. The first came forward and said, 'Lord, your ten pounds has made ten more pounds.' He said to him, 'Well done, good servant! Because you have been trustworthy in a very small thing, take charge of ten cities.' Then the second came, saying, 'Lord, your five pounds has made five more.' He said to him, 'And you, rule over five cities.' And another said, "Lord, your one pound has made two'; and so it went until another came, saying, 'Lord, here is your pound. I wrapped it up in a napkin, for I was afraid of you, because you are a harsh man; you take what you did not deposit, and reap what you did not sow.' He said to him, 'Out of your own mouth I will judge you, you wicked servant! You knew that I was a harsh man, taking what I did not deposit and reaping what I did not sow? Why then did you not put my money into the bank? Then when I returned I could at least have collected it with interest.'

"To the bystanders listening, he said, 'Take the pound from him and give it to the one who has ten pounds.' And they said to him, 'But, Lord, he has ten pounds!' But he said, 'I tell you, to all those who have, more will be given; but from those who have nothing, even what they have will be taken away. Now throw this worthless servant into the outer darkness, where men and women shall weep and gnash their teeth. But as for these enemies of mine who did not want me to be king over them—bring them here and slaughter them in my presence.'

"Therefore, keep awake yourselves, for otherwise, he may find you asleep when he comes suddenly. Take heed, keep alert; for you do not know when the time will come. And what I say to you I say to all: Keep awake."

45   Concerning true devotion

Jesus, seeing a poor widow drop her coins into the Temple Treasury, said, "Indeed, I tell you, this poor widow has put in more than all of those others who are contributing to the Treasury. For all of them have given out of their abundance; but she out of her poverty has put in everything she had, her whole living."

46   A prophecy about coming ages and the conclusion of temporal creation

Jesus, when the disciples asked about the coming of His Kingdom, said, "Beware that you are not led astray. For many will come in my name, saying, 'I am He! I am the Messiah!' and they will indeed lead many astray. And you will hear of wars and tumults and rumors of wars; see that you are not alarmed, for this must take place, but the end is not yet. For nation will rise against nation, and kingdom against kingdom, and there will be great signs from heaven, and famines, pestilence, and earthquakes in various places: all this is but the beginning of the birth pangs.

"Then they will hand you over to be tortured and will put you to death, and you will be hated by all nations because of my name. At that time, many will fall away, and they will kill one another and hate one another. And many false prophets will rise up and lead many astray. And because of the increase of wickedness and lawlessness, the love of many will grow cold. But the one who endures to the end will be saved. And the gospel will be proclaimed throughout the world, as a testimony to all the nations; and then the end will come.

"So when you see the desolating sacrilege where it ought not to be, as was spoken of by the prophet Daniel (let the reader understand) and when you see armies surrounding Jerusalem and standing in the holy place, then those in Judea must flee to the mountains; let not anyone who is on the housetop go down into his house to rescue his possessions; the one in the field must not turn back to get a coat. Woe to those who are pregnant and to those who are nursing infants in those days! Pray that your flight may not be in winter or on a Sabbath. For great distress shall fall upon the earth and wrath upon this people; they shall fall by the edge of the sword and be led captive among all nations; and Jerusalem will be stomped underfoot by Gentiles until the time of the Gentiles shall be fulfilled. But before that time there will be such great suffering as has not been from the beginning of creation until now, no, and never will be. And if those days had not been cut short, no one would be saved; but for the sake of the elect those days will be cut short.

"In the days after that tribulation, the sun will be darkened, and the moon will not give its light; the stars of heaven will fall, and upon the earth there will be the distress of nations in perplexity at the roaring of the sea and waves, men fainting with fear and anxiety over what is coming on the world, for the powers of heaven will be shaken. Then the sign of the Son of Man will appear in heaven, and then all the tribes of the earth will mourn, and they will see the Son of Man coming in the clouds with great power and glory. And he will send out his angels with a loud trumpet call, and they will gather his elect together from the four winds, from the farthest parts of the earth and from one end of heaven to the other. Now when these things begin to take place, look up and lift up your heads, because your redemption is drawing near."

47   Concerning the exact time of the end

Jesus, while resting a while on the Mount of Olives with His disciples, said, "Look at the fig tree and all the other trees and from them learn a lesson. As soon as the branches become tender and put forth leaves, you know that summer is near. In like manner, you, when you see all these things, must know that he is near, at the very gates, and that the Kingdom of God is near. Truly I tell you, this generation will not pass away until all these things have taken place. Heaven and earth will pass away, but my words will not pass away.

"But about that day and hour no one knows, neither the angels of heaven, nor the Son, but only the Father. Be careful that your hearts are not weighed down with dissipation and drunkenness and the worries of this life, and that day does not catch you suddenly like a trap. For it will come like a snare upon all who live on the face of the whole earth. Be watchful, therefore, at all times praying that you may have the strength to escape all these things that will take place, and to stand before the Son of Man."

48   The parable of holy watchfulness in anticipating the Kingdom

Jesus, in teaching the disciples, said, "Then the kingdom of heaven will be likened to ten virgins who took their lamps and went out to meet the bridegroom. Now, five of them were foolish and five were wise. Those who were foolish took their lamps, but they took no oil with them; but the wise took oil in their flasks with their lamps. But while the bridegroom was delayed, all of them became drowsy and slept. And at midnight there was a great cry, 'Look! Here the bridegroom is coming! Come out to meet him.' Then all of them got up and trimmed their lamps. The foolish said to the wise, 'Give us some of your oil, for our lamps are going out.' But the wise replied, 'No, lest there not be enough for you and for us; but go rather to the dealers and buy some for yourselves.' And while they went to buy it, the bridegroom came, and those who were ready went with him into the wedding; and the door was shut. Later the other five came also, saying, 'Lord, lord, open to us.' But he replied, 'Truly I tell you, I do not know you.' Keep awake therefore, for you know neither the day nor the hour."

49   The description of the final judgment

Jesus, instructing the disciples, said, "When the Son of Man comes in his glory, and all the holy angels with him, then he will sit on the throne of his glory. All the nations will be gathered before him, and he will separate them one from another as a shepherd separates his sheep from the goats, and he will put the sheep at his right hand but the goats at his left. Then the king will say to those at his right hand, 'Come, you blessed of my Father, inherit the kingdom prepared for you from the foundation of the world; for I was hungry and you gave me food, I was thirsty and you gave me drink, I was a stranger and you took me in, I was naked and you clothed me, I was sick and you ministered to me, I was in prison and you visited me.' Then the righteous will answer him, 'Lord, when was it that we saw you hungry and gave you food, or thirsty and gave you something to drink? And when was it that we saw you a stranger and took you in, or naked and gave you clothing? And when was it that we saw you sick or in prison and came to you?' And the king will answer them, 'Truly I tell you, just as you did it to one of the least of these my family, so you did it to me.'

"Then he will say to those at his left hand, 'Depart from me, you cursed ones. Depart from me into the eternal fire prepared for the devil and his angels; for I was hungry and you gave me no food, I was thirsty and you gave me no drink, I was a stranger and you did not take me in, naked and you did not clothe me, sick and in prison and you did not come to me.' Then they also will answer, 'Lord, when did we see you hungry or thirsty or a stranger or naked or sick or in prison, and did not care for you?' Then he will answer them, 'Truly I tell you, just as you did not do it to one of the least of these, you did not do it to me.' And these will go away into everlasting punishment, but the righteous into eternal life."

50   His farewell before crucifixion

Jesus, gathering them to Him on the Mount of Olives, said, "I am the true vine, and my Father is the keeper of the vineyard. Every branch in me that does not bear fruit, He takes away. Every branch that bears fruit He prunes to make it bear more fruit. You have already been made clean by the word that I have spoken to you. Abide in me as I abide in you. Just as the branch cannot bear fruit by itself unless it abides in the vine, neither can you unless you abide in me. I am the vine, you are the branches. Those who abide in me and I in them bear much fruit, because apart from me you can do nothing. Whoever does not abide in me is thrown out like a branch and is withered; and men gather them and throw them into the fire, and they are burned. My Father is glorified by this, that you bear much fruit; so you will be my disciples. As the Father has loved me, so have I loved you; abide in my love. If you keep my commandments, you will abide in my love, even as I have kept my Father's commandments and abide in His love. I have said these things to you so that my joy may be in you, and that your joy may be complete."

BOOK III

The Words of Healing Dialogue

1   The first healing miracle

Jesus, when asked by a nobleman in Capernaum to come and heal his desperately ill son, said, "Unless you see signs and wonders, you will not believe."

Jesus, when the nobleman continued to plead with Him, said, "Go on your way. Your son lives."

2   The first healing on a Sabbath and His response to public condemnation by religious leaders

Jesus, upon seeing a man who had been crippled for thirty-eight years lying by the pool of Bethesda, said, "Do you wish to be made whole?"

Jesus, when the man asked for His help, said, "Get up, pick up your bed, and walk."

Jesus, when He saw the man later in the Temple, said, "Consider, you are healed now. Go forth and sin no more, lest a worse thing befall you."

Jesus, when the Jews began to criticize Him for healing on **the Sabbath**, said, "My Father is working, and so am I."

3   The first exorcism

Jesus, rebuking an evil spirit that was tormenting a man, said, "Be silent and come out of him!"

4   First attempt to contain notoriety

Jesus, when asked by a leper if He would be willing to heal him, said, "I do choose. Be made clean! But see that you say nothing to anyone; rather go, show yourself to the priest, and offer for your cleansing what Moses commanded, as a proof to the people and as a testimony to them."

5   First healing of a Gentile

Jesus, when approached by an emissary to come and heal a centurion's sick servant, said, " I will come and heal him."

Jesus, in speaking of the Roman centurion's belief in Him, said "Truly I say to you, not even in Israel have I found such faith.

"I tell you, many will come from east and west and will eat with Abraham and Isaac and Jacob and all the prophets in the kingdom of heaven, while you yourselves, the heirs of the kingdom, will be thrust out; for behold, some are last who will be first, and some are first who will be last."

Jesus, sending instructions to the centurion, said, "Go; let it be done for you according to your faith."

6   The casting out of an objectively operative demon

Jesus, when one possessed of a demon asked healing from Him, first said to the demon, "Come out of the man, you unclean spirit!" and then asked, "What is your name?"

Jesus, to the demon who begged release into a herd of swine, said, "Go!" and to the man freed from demonic possession, said, "Go home to your friends and tell them how much the Lord has done for you, and how he has had mercy on you."

7   A direct absolution certified by a concomitant healing miracle

Jesus, when a paralytic was laid at His feet, said to the sick man, "Take heart, my son. Your sins are forgiven you."

Jesus, perceiving that those around the man questioned His authority to forgive sins, said to them, "Why do you question thus and think evil in your hearts? Which is easier: to say to the paralytic, 'Your sins are forgiven you?' or to say, 'Rise, take up your pallet and walk?'

"But that you may know that the Son of Man has authority on earth to forgive sins," He said, turning to the paralytic, "I say to you, rise, take up your bed, and go home."

8   The flow of power by proximity and without intention

Jesus, sensing that someone seeking miraculous healing had reached out to touch Him, first said, "Who touched me? Who touched my clothes? Someone has touched me, for I perceive that power has gone forth from me."

Jesus, when a woman came forward to admit she had indeed touched Him for healing, said, "Daughter, take heart. Your faith has made you whole. Go in peace and be healed of your disease."

9   A resuscitation

Jesus, summoned by a ruler of the synagogue to come lay hands on his daughter who had just died, said, "Do not fear, only believe, and she shall be well."

Jesus, to the mourners gathered outside the ruler's house, said, "Why do you make a tumult and weep? Depart, for the girl is not dead but sleeping."

Jesus, entering the house, took the girl by the hand and said, "*Talitha cumi*. Little girl, I say to you, arise."

10   Belief and faith as a measure of efficacy

Jesus, upon being followed by two blind men begging for His attention, said, "What do you want me to do for you?"

Jesus, being told they wished to see, said, "Do you believe I am able to do this?"

Jesus, upon hearing their confession of belief, touched their eyes and said, "According to your faith, be it done to you."

Jesus, in leaving them, said, "See that no one knows of this."

11   The correct interpretation of the Sabbath

Jesus, entering the synagogue on the Sabbath, saw a man with a withered hand and said, "Come and stand here."

Jesus, to the religious watching Him, said, "Is it lawful to heal on the Sabbath? Is it lawful to do good or to do harm? To save life or to kill? Suppose one of you has only one sheep and it falls into a pit on the Sabbath; will you not grab hold of it and lift it out? How much more valuable is a human being than a sheep! So it is lawful to do good on the Sabbath."

Jesus, grieved by their hardness of heart, turned to the man and said, "Stretch out your hand."

12   The compassionate raising of the widow's child

Jesus, passing a funeral procession in Nain and seeing the dead man's mother weeping there, said, "Do not weep."

Jesus, approaching the bier and touching the corpse, said, " Young man, I say to you arise."

13   An extended commentary on principalities and powers in the kingdom of Evil

Jesus, realizing that the religious leaders watching Him thought that He was casting out demons with the help of Beelzebul, turned to them and said, "How can Satan cast out Satan? Every kingdom divided against itself is laid waste; and if a city or a house is divided against itself, it will not be able to stand. If Satan casts out Satan, he is divided against himself; how then will his kingdom stand? He cannot stand and is coming to an end.

"If I cast out demons by Beelzebul, by whom do your own sons and exorcists cast them out? Therefore they will be your judges. But if it is by the Spirit and finger of God that I cast out demons, then the Kingdom of God has come upon you.

"Or how can one enter a strong man's house and plunder his property without first tying up the strong man? Then indeed the house can be plundered. When a strong man, fully armed, keeps watch over his house, his goods are safe; but when one who is more powerful attacks that man and overcomes him, then the victor takes away the man's armor and divides the spoils. Whoever is not with me is against me, and whoever does not gather with me scatters.

"Therefore I tell you, people will be forgiven for every sin and blasphemy, but blasphemy against the Spirit will not be forgiven. Whoever speaks a word against the Son of Man will be forgiven, but whoever speaks against the Holy Spirit will not be forgiven, either in this age or in the age to come, for he or she is guilty of an eternal sin."

14   His acknowledgment of a Gentile's faith

Jesus, when asked by His disciples to heal the demon-possessed daughter of a Gentile woman, said, "I was sent only to the lost sheep of Israel. Let the children be fed first, for it is not fair to take the children's food and throw it to the dogs."

Jesus, when the woman protested that even dogs were allowed to eat the children's fallen crumbs, said,

"O woman, great is your faith! For saying that, may it be done for you just as you desire. Go—the demon has left your daughter."

15   The healing of the deaf mute

Jesus, when the crowd brought Him a deaf mute, took the man aside, touched his ears and his tongue, and said, "Ephphatha. Be opened."

16   The healing of the blind man

Jesus, laying His hands in healing on the eyes of a blind man, said, "Do you see anything?"

Jesus, once the man saw clearly, told him to go to his own home and said, "Neither go into the village nor tell anyone in the town."

17   Faith as a linchpin

Jesus, finding His disciples engaged in conversation with the crowds, said, "What were you discussing with them?"

Jesus, being told by one of the crowd that the disciples had been unable to cure his demon-possessed son, said, "O you faithless and perverse generation! How long am I to be with you? How long must I suffer you? Bring him here to me."

Jesus, when the possessed boy had been brought to Him, turned to the father and said, "How long has he had this?"

Jesus, besought earnestly by the father for help said, "If you can believe, all things are possible, because all things are possible to those who believe."

Jesus then said, "You dumb and deaf spirit, I command you: Come out of him and never enter into him again."

18 The reason for some instances of human debility

Jesus, when asked whose fault it was that a nearby beggar had been born blind, said, "Neither this man nor his parents sinned; he was born blind so that the works of God might be revealed in him. I must work the works of Him Who sent me while it is day; for night is coming, when no one can work. As long as I am in the world, I am the light of the world."

Jesus, turning to the blind beggar, said, "Go, wash in the pool of Siloam."

Jesus, when He heard that the beggar had been thrown out of the synagogue because he had been healed on the Sabbath, sought the man out and said, "Do you believe in the Son of Man?"

Jesus, when the healed beggar asked who the Son of Man was, said, "You have both seen him, and it is he who is speaking with you."

Jesus, receiving the man's confession of faith, said, "I came into this world for judgment so that those who do not see may see, and those who do see may become blind."

Jesus, when the Pharisees who overheard Him protested that they surely were not blind, said, "If you were blind, you would not have sin. But now you say, 'We see.' Therefore, your sin remains."

19   His use of two unsolicited healings for Sabbath teaching

Jesus, one Sabbath when He was teaching in the synagogue, saw a woman who had been crippled for years and, turning to her, said, "Woman, you are freed from your infirmity."

Jesus, castigated by the synagogue leaders because He had healed on the Sabbath, turned to them and said, "You hypocrites! Which one of you does not untie his ox or his donkey from the manger and lead it away in order to give it water on the Sabbath day? And ought not this woman, a daughter of Abraham whom Satan bound for eighteen long years, be loosed from this bondage on the Sabbath day?"

Jesus, when He was eating one Sabbath day at the home of a Pharisee, saw a man with dropsy and, turning to His host, said, "Is it lawful to cure people on the Sabbath, or not?"

Jesus, when no one answered Him, said, "Which of you, having a son or an ox that has fallen into a well, will you not immediately pull him out on a Sabbath day?"

20   The role of faith in the healing of the Gentile leper

Jesus, as He passed ten lepers who begged Him to cure them, turned to them and said, "Go and show yourselves to the priests."

Jesus, when one of the ten, a Samaritan, came running back to Him in thanksgiving, said, "Were there not ten of you made clean? The other nine, where are they?

Was not one of them found to return and give praise to God except this foreigner?"

Jesus, looking upon the Samaritan at His feet, said, "Get up and go on your way; your faith has made you whole."

21　The pivotal efficacy of faith in healing

Jesus, when a blind man named Bartimaeus called out to Him from the roadside, to His disciples said, "Call him," and to the man, "What would you have me do for you?"

Jesus, when Bartimaeus asked for his sight to be restored, said, "Receive your sight and go your way, for your faith has made you whole."

BOOK IV

The Words of Intimate Conversation

1   The first saying

Jesus, when His anxious parents found Him in the Temple studying, said, "How is it that you sought me? Did you not know that I must be in my father's house?"

2   First recorded exchange with His cousin, John the Baptizer

Jesus, when John the Baptizer expressed reservations about baptizing Him, said, "Let it be so now; for thus it is fitting for us to fulfill all righteousness."

IV

3   The desert temptations

Jesus, when tempted by Satan to turn the desert stones into bread, said, "It is written, 'Man shall not live by bread alone, but by every word that proceeds from the mouth of God.'"

Jesus, when tempted by Satan to prove His divinity by throwing Himself off the parapet of the Temple, said, "Again it is written, 'You shall not tempt the Lord your God.'"

Jesus, when offered the whole world if only He would bow to Satan, said, "Begone, Satan! For it is written, 'You shall worship the Lord your God, and Him only shall you serve.'"

4   The calling of Philip and Nathaniel

Jesus, on His way to Galilee, passed Philip and said, "Follow me."

Jesus, when Philip brought Nathaniel to Him, said, "Behold, an Israelite indeed, in whom there is no guile."

Jesus, when asked by Nathaniel how He could possibly know anything about him, said, "Before Philip even called you and while you were still under the fig tree, I saw you."

Jesus, when Nathaniel declared that He must be the Messiah, said, "Do you believe that because I said I saw you under the fig tree? You will see greater things than that. Yes, I say most surely, after this you will see heaven open and the angels of God ascending and descending upon the Son of Man."

5   With His mother at a wedding in Cana

Jesus, when asked by His mother to provide more wine for His host at a wedding they were attending in Cana, said, "Woman, what have I to do with you? My hour is not yet come."

Jesus, then turning to servants, said, "Fill up the waters jugs with water. Then draw out from them and carry what you have to the director of the feast."

6   The calling of James and John

Jesus, passing by James and John at their boat, said, "Follow me, and I will make you become fishers of men."

7   About the correct use of present time

Jesus, when urged by His disciples to eat instead of teaching the crowd, said, "I have food to eat that you know nothing about; for my food is to do the will of Him who sent me and to complete His work. Do you not say, 'Four months more, then the harvest will come'? But I tell you, look around you, and see how the fields already are ripe for harvesting. The reaper is already receiving wages and is gathering fruit for eternal life, so that sower and reaper may rejoice together. For here the saying holds true, 'One sows and another reaps.' I sent you to reap that for which you did not labor. Others have labored, and you have entered into their labor."

8   The beginning of the public ministry

Jesus, gathering His disciples to commence their ministry, said, "Let us go on to the next towns and other cities also, so I can preach there; for it is for this reason that I was sent."

9   About becoming fishers of men

Jesus, as soon as He had finished addressing the people from Simon's boat, turned to Simon and said, "Put out into the deep and let down your nets for a catch."

Jesus, when the disciples were frightened by the great size of the catch He had told them to cast for, said, "Do not be afraid. Henceforth you will be catching men."

10   Faith as a force in the physical realm

Jesus, speaking one day to His disciples, said, "Let us go across to the other side of the lake."

Jesus, when the boat began to swamp and the disciples to panic, said to the sea, "Peace, be still!" and to the disciples, "Where is your faith and why, O men of little faith, are you afraid?"

11   His description to the emissaries from John the Baptizer, of His early, public ministry

Jesus, speaking to emissaries from John the Baptizer, said, "Go and tell John what you hear and see: that the blind receive their sight, the lame walk, the lepers are cleansed, the deaf hear, the dead are raised, and the poor have good news brought to them. And blessed is anyone who takes no offense at me."

12   The importance of rest

Jesus, after the disciples had returned from their evangelizing trip, said, "Come away to a deserted place all by yourselves and rest a while."

13   His engagement of Philip in the feeding of the thousands

Jesus, seeing a great crowd gathered around Him, called His disciples to Him and said, "I have compassion for this multitude, because they have been with me now for three days and have nothing to eat. If I send them away hungry to their homes, they will faint on the way—and some of them have come from a great distance."

Jesus, turning to Philip, said, "Where shall we find bread enough for all these people to eat?"

Jesus, when none of the disciples could answer His question, then said, "They need not go away. You give them something to eat. How many loaves do you have? Go and see. Make the people sit down in companies of fifty, and bring the loaves to me."

Jesus, once the crowd was fully fed, said, "Gather up the scraps that remain, so that nothing will be lost."

14   Another demonstration of faith as a primal force in the physical world

Jesus, walking across the sea toward the boat in which His disciples were, said, "Be of good cheer! It is I. Do not be afraid."

Jesus, asked by Peter for permission to approach Him across the waters, said, "Come!"

Jesus, when Peter began to flounder, reached out to him and said, "O man of little faith! Why did you doubt?"

15   His claiming of kingship on earth as well as in Heaven

Jesus, talking with His disciples, said, "Who do people say I am? Who do they say that the Son of Man is?"

Jesus, once he had heard their answers, said, "But who do you say that I am?"

Jesus, so soon as Simon Peter had answered, "You are the Messiah, the Son of the living God," said, "Blessed are you, Simon son of Jonah! For flesh and blood have not revealed this to you, but by my Father Who is in heaven. And I tell you, you are Peter, and on this rock I will build my church, and the gates of Hades will not prevail against it. I will give you the keys of the kingdom of heaven, and whatever you bind on earth will be bound in heaven, and whatever you loose on earth will be loosed in heaven."

16   His correcting of Peter

Jesus, in cautioning His disciples about His approaching death, said, "The Son of Man must undergo great suffering, and be rejected by the elders, chief priests, and scribes, and be killed, and on the third day be raised from the dead."

Jesus, when Peter rebuked Him for such teachings, said, "Get behind me, Satan! For you are a hindrance to me and on the side not of God but of men!"

17   His instructions regarding His transfiguration

Jesus, after He was transfigured in the presence of Peter, James, and John, touched them and said, "Rise, and have no fear."

Jesus, as they were leaving, said, "Tell no one about the vision until the Son of Man is raised from the dead."

18   A prophecy of His death and Resurrection

Jesus, in warning His disciples, said, "Let these words sink into your ears: The Son of Man is to be delivered into the hands of men and they will kill him; and when he is killed, after three days he will be raised."

19   The proper conduct of believers in relation to temporal government

Jesus, when Simon Peter came into the house, said, "What do you think, Simon? From whom do the rulers and kings of the earth take toll and tribute? From their sons or from other people?"

Jesus, when Peter had answered that kings did not tax their own, said, "Then the sons are free. Nevertheless, so as not to give offense to them, go to the sea and cast your hook, and take the first fish that strikes. When you open its mouth, you will find a shekel. Take that and give it to the tax collectors for you and for me."

20   The definition of greatness in the Kingdom

Jesus, near the end of a walking tour with His disciples, said, "What were you discussing on the way here?"

Jesus, upon being told they were discussing who is greatest in the Kingdom of Heaven, called a child to Him and said, "Unless you turn and become like children, you will never enter the kingdom of heaven. Whoever becomes humble like this child is the greatest in the kingdom of heaven; and whoever receives one such child in my name welcomes me; for the person who is least among you all is the greatest one."

21   The power of His name as nonproprietary

Jesus, upon being told by His disciples that a stranger was healing in His name, said, "Do not forbid him. Nobody who does a mighty work in my name will be able to say ill of me later; for anyone who is not against us is for us. Anyone who gives you a drink of water in my name because you belong to me, I tell you most truly, will by no means lose his or her reward."

22   The use of holy or divine power

Jesus, when asked by the disciples if they should call fire from heaven upon some Samaritans who forbade Him entrance into their village, said, "You do not know what manner of spirit you are of! The Son of Man did not come to destroy people's lives, but to save them."

23   On proper timing

Jesus, upon being urged by His brothers to go up to Jerusalem to make His presence known, said, "My time has not yet come, though your time is always here. The world cannot hate you, but it hates me because I testify against it that its works are evil. Go to the festival yourselves. I am not going up yet to this festival, for my time has not yet fully come."

24   The chastising of Martha

Jesus, when asked by Martha to order her sister Mary to help with serving their guests, said, "Martha, Martha, you are anxious and troubled by many things; but one thing is needed. Mary has chosen that good part, which will not be taken from her."

25   His message to Herod concerning His approaching death

Jesus, upon being told that He should leave because Herod wanted to kill Him, said, "Go and tell that fox for me, 'Listen, I cast out demons and perform cures today and tomorrow, and on the third day I will be finished. Nevertheless, I must be on my journey today, tomorrow, and the next day, for it cannot be that a prophet should be killed outside of Jerusalem.'"

26   The raising of Lazarus

Jesus, when He heard that His friend Lazarus was ill at his home in Bethany, said, "This sickness is not unto death; rather it is for the glory of God, so that the Son of God may be glorified through it."

Jesus, two days later, gathered the disciples and said, "Let us go into Judea again."

Jesus, when they protested the danger of going so near Jerusalem again, said, "Are there not twelve hours in the day? Anyone who walks during the day does not stumble, because he sees the light of this world. But those who walk at night stumble, because there is no light in them.

"Our friend Lazarus has fallen asleep, but I am going there to awaken him."

Jesus, when the disciples protested that sleep was good for the ill, said, "Lazarus is dead. And I am glad, for your sakes, that I was not there, so that you may believe. But let us go to him."

Jesus, when He arrived in Bethany and found that Lazarus had been in the tomb for four days, turned to his sisters and said, "Your brother will rise again."

Jesus, when Martha told Him that she knew her brother would rise again in the resurrection on the last day, said, "I am the resurrection and the life. He that believes in me, even though he were dead, yet will he live; and everyone who lives and believes in me will never die. Do you believe this?"

Jesus said, "Where have you laid him?"

Jesus, coming to the tomb, said, "Take away the stone."

Jesus, when Martha protested that the stench would overwhelm them, said, "Did I not tell you that if you believed, you would see the glory of God?"

Jesus, looking up to heaven, said, "Father, I thank You for having heard me. I knew that You always hear me, but for the sake of those standing here, I have said this, so that they may believe that You sent me."

Jesus, with a loud cry, said, "Lazarus, come forth!"

Jesus, seeing Lazarus emerge still wrapped in grave-clothes, said, "Unbind him, and let him go."

27   Children as examples of necessary innocence

Jesus, when His disciples tried to move some children away from Him, rebuked them and said, "Let the little children come to me, and do not hinder them; for it is to such as these that the Kingdom of God belongs. Truly I tell you, unless you turn and become like children, you will never enter the Kingdom of God; for whoever does not receive the Kingdom of God like a little child will never enter it."

28   His second specific prophecy to the twelve of His forthcoming death

Jesus, taking the twelve aside, said, "Behold, we are going up to Jerusalem, and everything that has been written by the prophets about the Son of Man will be accomplished. The Son of Man will be handed over to the chief priests and the scribes, and they will condemn him to death; then they will hand him over to the Gentiles; they will mock him, and treat him shamefully, and spit upon him, and flog him, and crucify him; and after three days he will rise again."

29   Concerning the Father's authority over the Son's followers

Jesus, when James and John and their mother approached Him in private, said, "What would you have me do for you?"

Jesus, when told that they wanted Him to grant the two disciples the places of greatest honor in His coming

Kingdom, said, "You have no idea what you are asking. Are you able to drink the cup that I am to drink, or be baptized with the baptism with which I am baptized?"

Jesus, when they told Him they were, said, "The cup that I drink you will indeed drink; and with the baptism with which I am baptized you shall be baptized; but to sit at my right hand or at my left is not mine to grant, for it will be given to those for whom it has been prepared by my Father."

30   The redemption of Zacchaeus

Jesus, when He passed under a sycamore that Zacchaeus, a tax collector, had climbed in order to see Him better, looked up and said, "Zacchaeus, make haste and come down, for I must stay at your house today."

Jesus, when after supper He saw Zacchaeus's repentance for his former fraudulent deeds, said, "Today salvation has come to this house, since he also is a son of Abraham; for the Son of Man came to seek and to save that which was lost."

31   Instructions preparatory to the Triumphal Entry into Jerusalem

Jesus, nearing Bethphage and the Mount of Olives, turned to two of the disciples and said, "Go into the village ahead of you, and immediately as you enter it you will find a donkey tied, and a colt with her; untie them and bring them to me. If anyone says anything to you, just say this, 'The Lord needs them, and will send them back immediately.'"

32   His acknowledgment of His popularity

Jesus, when the Pharisees told Him to restrain the crowds rejoicing around Him, said, "I tell you, if these were silent, the very stones would cry out."

33   About the Holy City

Jesus, approaching Jerusalem, wept over the city and said, "If you had known, even you, especially on this day, the things that make for your peace! But now they are hidden from your eyes. Indeed, the days will come upon you when your enemies will dig a trench around you and surround you, and hem you in on every side. They will level you to the ground, you and your children within you, and they will leave within you not one stone upon another; because you did not recognize the time of your visitation."

34   The beginning of the days of final judgment

Jesus, when the disciples came saying that certain Greeks had come to the city and wanted to meet Him, said, "The hour has come for the Son of Man to be glorified. Most earnestly I tell you, unless a grain of wheat falls into the earth and dies, it remains alone; but if it dies, it bears much fruit. Whoever serves me must follow me, and where I am, there will my servant be also. Whoever serves me, the Father will honor. Now my soul is troubled. And what should I say—'Father, save me from this hour'? But it is for this purpose that I have come to this hour. Father, glorify Your name."

Jesus, when a voice was heard from heaven saying. "I have glorified it, and I will glorify it again," said, "This voice did not come for my sake, but for yours. Now is the judgment of this world; now the ruler of this world will be driven out. And I, if I am lifted up from the earth, will draw all peoples to myself. The light is with you for a little longer. Walk while you have the light, so that the darkness may not overtake you. If you walk in the darkness, you do not know where you are going. While you have the light, believe in the light, so that you may become children of light."

35   Another conversation about faith as a physical agent

Jesus, when He was hungry, passed a fig tree by the roadside, but when he saw that it had no fruit, He turned to it and said, "May no fruit ever come from you again and may no one ever eat from you again."

Jesus, when they passed the cursed tree the next morning and found it withered, turned to the disciples and said, "Have faith in God. Truly, I tell you, if you say to this mountain, 'Be uprooted and thrown into the sea,' and you do not doubt in your heart but believe that what you say will come to pass, it will be done for you. So I tell you, whatever you ask for in prayer, believe that you have received it, and it will be yours."

36   A prophecy about the destruction of the Temple

Jesus, when His disciples called His attention to the beauty of the Temple, said, "You see all of these great buildings, do you not? But as for these things that you see, truly I tell you, the days will come when there will not be one stone left upon another that will not be torn down."

37   Concerning the time of His approaching crucifixion

Jesus, in preparing His disciples, said, "You know that in two days the Passover is coming and the Son of Man will be delivered up to be crucified."

38   The use of extravagant devotion

Jesus, when a female disciple was criticized for pouring an expensive aromatic oil on Him as He sat at table, said, "Let her alone; why do you trouble her? She has done a good work for me. For you have the poor always with you, and you can show them kindness whenever you wish; but you will not always have me. In pouring this ointment on my body, she has done what she could; she has anointed my body beforehand for its burial. And truly I tell you, wherever the gospel is proclaimed in the whole world, what this woman has done will be told as a memorial to her."

39   Instructions about their last meal together

Jesus, speaking with two of His disciples about the approaching Passover, said, "Go and prepare the Passover that we may eat. Go into the city, and a man carrying a jar of water will meet you; follow him, and wherever he enters, say to the owner of the house, 'The Teacher says, "My time is at hand. Where is the guest room where I may eat the Passover with my disciples?"' Then he will show you a large upper room, furnished and prepared. Make ready for us there."

40   Final instruction about servant leadership

Jesus, when challenged by Peter because He had begun washing the disciples' feet as they sat at table, said, "You do not know now what I am doing, but later you will understand; for unless I wash you, you can have no share with me."

Jesus, when Simon then asked to be washed completely, said, "Anyone who has bathed does not need washing, except for his or her feet, for he is entirely cleaned already. And you are clean, although not all of you."

Jesus, when He had finished washing their feet, sat down amongst them and said, "Do you understand what I have just done to you? You call me Teacher and Lord—and so you should, for that is what I am. If therefore, I, your Lord and Teacher, have washed your feet, you also ought to wash one another's feet. For I have given you an example, that you should do as I have done to you. Truly, servants are not greater than their master, nor are those sent greater than the one who sent them. And if you know these things, happy are you if you do them."

41   His direct instructions to them in preparation for His leaving them

Jesus, speaking to them at their last supper together, said, "I have spoken these things to you so that you might not stumble. They will put you out of the synagogues. Indeed, the time is coming when anyone who kills you will think that he or she is doing God's work. And they do this because they have not known the Father or me. But I have said these things to you so that when that time comes you may remember that I told you about them.

"I did not say these things to you from the beginning, because I was with you. But now I am going away to Him Who sent me; yet none of you asks me, 'Where are you going?' And because I have said these things to you, sorrow has filled your hearts. Nevertheless I tell you the truth: it is to your advantage that I go away, for if I do not go away, the Advocate and Comforter will not come to you; but if I go away, I will send Him to you. And when He comes, He will convince the world about sin and about righteousness and judgment: about sin, because they do not believe in me; about righteousness, because I am going to the Father and you will see me no longer; about judgment, because the ruler of this world has been condemned.

"I still have many things to say to you, but you cannot bear them now. When the Spirit of truth comes, He will guide you into all the truth; for He will not speak on His own authority, but will speak whatever He hears, and He will declare to you the things that are to come. He will glorify me, because He will take what is mine and declare it to you. All that the Father has is mine. For this reason I said that He will take what is mine and declare it to you. A little while and you will no longer see me, and again a little while and you will see me."

Jesus, when the disciples began to whisper about what His meaning was, said. "Are you questioning among yourselves what I meant when I said, 'A little while and you will no longer see me, and again a little while and you will see me'? Truly, I tell you, you will weep and lament, but the world will rejoice; you will have pain, but your sorrow will turn into joy. When a woman is in labor she is in agony, because her hour has come. But as soon as her child is born, she no longer remembers the anguish because of the joy that a human being has been brought into the world. Just so, you have pain now; but I will see you again, and your hearts will rejoice, and no one will take your joy from you. And on that day you will ask me nothing; truly I tell you, whatever you ask the Father in my name, He will give it to you. Until now you have not asked for anything in my name. Ask and you will receive, so that your joy may be complete.

"I have told these things to you in metaphors. The hour is coming when I will no longer speak to you in figures of speech, but will tell you plainly of the Father. On that day you will ask in my name. I do not say to you that I will ask the Father on your behalf; for the Father Himself loves you, because you have loved me and have believed that I proceeded from God. I came forth from the Father and have come into the world; again, I am leaving the world and am going to the Father.

"Do you now believe? The hour is coming, indeed it has now come, when you will be scattered, everyone to his home, and you will leave me alone. Yet I am not alone because the Father is with me. I have said this to you so that in me you may have peace. In the world you face persecution. But be of good courage; I have conquered the world!"

42 The poignancy of betrayal and of human endings

Jesus, as He sat at the Passover table with His disciples, said, "Truly I tell you, I know whom I have chosen, yet one of you will betray me that the scripture might be fulfilled that says, 'He that eats with me has lifted up his heel against me.' Indeed, one who is eating with me, one of the twelve, one who is dipping bread into the bowl with me, will betray me, and I tell you this before it comes to pass so that you will know that I am He. For the Son of Man goes, as it is written of him, but woe to that one by whom the Son of Man is betrayed! It would have been better for that one not to have been born."

Jesus, when asked who it was that should betray Him, said, "It is he to whom I shall give a sop of bread when I have dipped it."

Jesus, asked by Judas if he were the one He meant, said, "You have said so. What you do, do quickly."

43 His words concerning the bread and wine

Jesus, turning to them, then said, "I have yearned to eat this Passover meal with you before I suffer; for I tell you I shall no longer eat of it until it is fulfilled in the Kingdom of God."

Jesus, as He broke the Passover bread, said, "Take this and divide it among yourselves and eat, for this is my body which is given for you. Do this in remembrance of me."

Jesus, taking a cup, said, "Drink you all from it, for this is my blood of the new covenant, which is poured out for many for the forgiveness of sins. I tell you, I will never again drink of the fruit of the vine until the day when I drink it new with you in the Kingdom of God."

44   Instructions about the employment of worldly goods in the work of the Kingdom

Jesus, talking to them at the Passover meal, said, "When I sent you out without a purse or bag or sandals, did you lack for anything?"

Jesus, when they said they had lacked for nothing, then said, "But now, let anyone who has a purse, take it, and likewise a bag. And the one who has no sword must sell his cloak and buy one. For I tell you, this scripture must be fulfilled in me: 'And he was reckoned among the lawless.' And indeed what is written about me is being fulfilled."

Jesus, when they said they had two swords with them, "It is enough."

45   The new commandment

Jesus, as soon as Judas had left the upper room, turned to them and said, "Now is the Son of Man glorified, and God glorified in him. And if God has been glorified in him, God will also glorify him in Himself and will glorify him at once. Little children, I am with you only a short while longer. You will look for me; and as I said to the Jews so now I say to you, 'Where I am going, you cannot come.' But I give you a new commandment: that you love one another. Just as I have loved you, so also you should love one another. By this all will know that you are my disciples, if you have love for one another.

"This is my commandment, that you love one another as I have loved you. Greater love has no man than that he lay down his life for a friend's. You are my friends if you do what I command you. I no longer call you servants, because the servant does not know what the master is doing; but I have called you friends, because I have made known to you everything that I have heard from my Father. You did not choose me but I chose you. And I ordained you to go and bring forth fruit that will last, that whatever you ask of the Father in my name, He may give you. I am giving you these commands so that you may love one another.

"If the world hates you, you know that it hated me before it hated you. If you belonged to the world, the world would love its own. Because you are not of the world, for I have chosen you out of the world—therefore the world hates you. Remember the word that I said to you, 'Servants are not greater than their master.' If they have persecuted me, they will persecute you; if they have kept my word, they will keep yours also. But they will do all these things to you on account of my name, because they do not know Him who sent me. If I had not come and spoken to them, then they would not have sin; but now they have no way to cloak their sin. Whoever hates me hates my Father also. If I had not done among them works that no one else ever did, they would not have sin. But now they have seen and hated both me and my Father. But this comes to pass in order to fulfill the word that is written in their law, 'They hated me without a cause.'"

46 The prophecy about their weakness and failure in the face of fear

Jesus, cautioning them while they were still gathered in the upper room, said, "You will all stumble away because of me this night; for it is written, 'I will strike the shepherd, and the sheep of the flock will be scattered.' But after I am raised up, I will go ahead of you to Galilee."

Jesus, when Simon Peter said he would follow Him wherever He went, said, "Simon, Simon, where I go you cannot follow me now, but you will follow me afterward; for truly I tell you, Satan has indeed asked for you that he may sift you like wheat, but I have prayed for you that your own faith should not fail; and when you have returned to me, strengthen your brothers and sisters. For I tell you, Peter, the cock will not crow twice this day before you have three times denied that you know me."

47 His assertion of His salvific role

Jesus, speaking to those left at table, said, "Let not your hearts be troubled. You believe in God; believe also in me. In my Father's house there are many mansions. If it were not so, I would have told you, I go to prepare a place for you; and if I go and prepare a place for you, I will surely come again and take you unto myself, so that where I am, there you may be also. And you know both the place and the way where I am going; for I am the way, and the truth, and the life. No one comes to the Father except through me. If you know me, you will know my Father also. From now on you do know Him and have seen Him."

Jesus, when Philip asked Him to show them the Father, said, "Have I been so long a time with you, Philip, and still you do not know me? Whoever has seen me has seen the Father. How can you say, 'Show us the Father'? Do you not believe that I am in the Father and the Father is in me? The words that I say to you I do not speak on my own; but the Father Who dwells in me does His works. Believe me that I am in the Father and the Father is in me; but if you do not, then believe me because of the works themselves. Verily I tell you, the one who believes in me will also do the works that I do and, in fact, will do greater works than these, because I am going to the Father. I will do whatever you ask in my name, so that the Father may be glorified in the Son. If in my name you ask me for anything, I will do it."

48   The promise of the coming of the Comforter and Advocate

Jesus, looking around at those gathered at the Passover table, said, "If you love me, you will keep my commandments. And I will ask the Father, and He will give you another Advocate whom I will send to you from the Father and who will be with you forever, even the Spirit of truth, who proceeds from the Father and whom the world cannot receive, because it neither sees Him nor knows Him. He will testify on my behalf and you also will testify on my behalf, because you have been with me from the beginning. You know Him, because He abides with you, and He will be in you.

"I will not leave you comfortless and orphaned; I will come to you. In a little while the world will no longer see me, but you will see me; and because I live, you also will live. On that day you will know that I am in the Father, and you are in me, and I in you. They who have my commandments and keep them are those who love me; and those who love me will be loved by my Father, and I will love them and reveal myself to them. Those who love me will keep my words, and my Father will love them, and We will come to them and make our home with them. Whoever does not love me does not keep my words; and the word that you hear is not mine but is from the Father Who sent me. I have said these things to you while I am still with you. But the Comforter and Advocate, the Holy Spirit, will teach you everything, and remind you of all that I have said to you."

49   The benediction

Jesus, as the Passover meal was ending, said, "Peace I leave with you; my peace I give unto you. But not as the world gives do I give to you. Do not let your hearts be troubled, and do not let them be afraid. You heard me say to you, 'I am going away, and I am coming back again to you.' If you loved me, you would rejoice that I am going to the Father, because the Father is greater than I. From now on I will not talk much with you, for the ruler of this world is coming. He has no power over me; but I do

as the Father has commanded me so that the world may
know that I love the Father."

Jesus then said, "Arise, let us be on our way."

50   His last prayer before them

Jesus, when He was done speaking with the disciples,
raised His eyes to heaven and said, "Father, the hour has
come; glorify Your Son so that the Son may glorify You,
for You have given him authority over all people, to give
eternal life to all whom You have given him. And this
is eternal life, that they may know You, the only true
God, and Jesus, the Christ whom You have sent. I have
glorified You on earth, I have finished the work that You
gave me to do. So now, Father, glorify me in Your own
Self with the glory that I had in Your presence before the
world existed.

"I have made Your name known to those whom You
gave me out of the world. They were Yours, and You gave
them to me, and they have kept Your word. Now they
know that everything You have given me is from You;
for the words that You gave to me I have given to them,
and they have received them and know of a certainty that
I came from You; and they have believed that You did
indeed send me. I pray for them; I do not pray for the
world, but on behalf of those whom You have given me,
because they are Yours. All mine are Yours, and Yours
are mine; and I am glorified in them. And now I am no
more in the world, but they are in the world, and I am
coming to You.

"Holy Father, keep these whom You have given me
through Your name, so that they may be one, as we are

one. While I was with them, I protected them in the world, I kept in Your name those whom You had given me. I guarded them, and not one of them is lost except the son of perdition, in order that the scripture might be fulfilled. And now I come to You, and I speak these things in the world so that they may have my joy made complete in themselves. I have given them Your word, and the world has hated them because they are not of the world, just as I am not of the world. I do not ask that You take them out of the world, but I ask You to keep them from the evil. They do not belong to the world, just as I do not belong to the world. Make them holy in Your truth; Your word is truth. As You have sent me into the world, even so I have sent them into the world. And for their sakes I sanctify myself, so that they also may be sanctified in truth.

"I do not pray for these alone, but also on behalf of those who will believe in me through their word, that they may all be one. As you, Father, are in me and I am in You, so may they also be in Us, so that the world may believe that You have sent me. The glory that You have given me I have given them, so that they may be one, as We are one; I in them and You in me, that they may be made perfect in one and that the world may know that You have sent me and have loved them even as You have loved me. Father, I will that these also, whom You have given me, may be with me where I am, to see my glory, which You have given me because You loved me before the foundation of the world. Righteous Father, the world has not known You, but I have known You; and these have known that You have sent me. I have declared to them Your name and will declare it, so that the love with which You have loved me may be in them, and I in them."

51   In the garden of Gethsemane

Jesus, entering the Garden of Gethsemane, turned to the disciples and said, "Sit here and pray that you not enter into temptation, while I go over there and pray."

Jesus, then taking Peter, James, and John aside, said, "My soul is deeply sorrowful, even unto death. Stay here and watch with me."

Jesus, withdrawing a short way from the three, threw Himself on the ground and praying, said, "Abba, Father, if it is possible, let this cup pass from me; yet not my will but Your will be done."

Jesus, when He returned and found the three sleeping, said, "Simon, could you not watch with me for one hour? Stay awake and pray that you may not fall into temptation, for the spirit indeed is willing, but the flesh is weak."

Jesus, withdrawing from them again to pray, said, "My Father, if this cannot pass unless I drink it, Your will be done."

Jesus, when He returned the third time and found them sleeping again, said, "Are you still sleeping and taking your rest? See, the hour is at hand, and the Son of Man is betrayed into the hands of sinners. Get up, let us be going. See, my betrayer is at hand."

52   The arrest and His interpretation of it

Jesus, when the armed crowd came to seize Him, said, "Whom do you seek?"

Jesus, when they answered, "Jesus of Nazareth," said, "I am he."

Jesus, when He looked and saw Judas leading them, said, "Judas, why have you come? Would you betray the Son of Man with a kiss? Then, Friend, do what you are here to do."

Jesus, when the crowd pulled back in fear, again said, "Whom do you seek?"

Jesus, when they once more answered "Jesus of Nazareth," said, "I have told you that I am he. If you really seek me, then let these others go."

Jesus, when Peter then drew a sword and cut off the ear of one of the servants of the High Priest to defend Him, said, "No more of this!"

Jesus, touching and restoring the man's severed ear, turned to Peter and said, "Permit even this. Put your sword back into its sheath; for those who take up the sword will perish by the sword. Or do you think that I cannot appeal to my Father and He will at once provide me more than twelve legions of angels? But how then would the scriptures be fulfilled which say it must happen in this way; for the cup which my Father has given me is the cup I must drink."

Jesus then turned to the armed crowd and said, "Have you come out with swords and clubs to take me as though I were a bandit? Day after day I sat in the Temple teaching, and you did not arrest me. But this is your hour and of the power of darkness. All this has taken place so that the scriptures of the prophets may be fulfilled, and let it be so."

53 His claiming, before the High Priest, His divinity

Jesus, standing bound before the High Priest and being ordered to declare if He were or were not the Son of God, said, "I spoke openly in the world. I even taught in the synagogue and the Temple, where the religious always resort; and I have said nothing in secret. Why do you ask me about such? Ask those who heard me what I have said. Indeed, they know exactly what I have said. Yet if I tell you, you will not believe me. And if I ask you, you will not answer me. But you have said I am Son of God, and I am. And I tell you that henceforth you will see the Son of Man seated at the right hand of the power of God and coming with the clouds of heaven."

Jesus, when an officer of the court struck Him for His words, said, "If I have spoken evil, prove it. If not, why strike me?"

54 Testimony before Pilate

Jesus, when asked by Pilate, the governor, if He were King of the Jews, said, "You have said so; but did you say so of your own knowledge, or did others say it to you about me?"

Jesus, when Pilate said he knew nothing of Judaism and asked what He had done to so provoke His fellow citizens, said, "My kingdom is not of this world. If it were, then my servants would fight so that I would not be delivered over to the Jews; but for now my kingdom is not from here. You say I am a king. To this very end I was born and for this I came into the world, that I might bear witness to the truth. Everyone who is of the truth hears my voice."

Jesus, when asked by Pilate why He did not fear him, said, "You could have no power at all over me unless it were given to you from above. For that reason, those who delivered me into your power have the greater sin."

55 His prophecy about the end times

Jesus, taunted by the crowd following Him on the road to Golgatha, turned to them and said, "Daughters of Jerusalem, do not weep for me, but weep for yourselves and for your children. For the days are surely coming in which they will say, 'Blessed are the barren, and the wombs that never bore, and the breasts that never nursed.' Then they will begin to say to the mountains, 'Fall on us'; and to the hills, 'Cover us.' For if they do this when the wood is green, what will happen when it is dry?"

56 His words of forgiveness

Jesus, when they had nailed Him onto the cross, said, "Father, forgive them, for they know not what they are doing."

57 His assigning of John as caregiver to Mary

Jesus, when, from the cross, He saw His mother standing beside John, said, "Woman, behold your son."

Jesus, speaking to John, said, "Behold, your mother."

58 His resignation

Jesus, knowing all things had now been accomplished, said, "I thirst."

59 His granting of salvation to one of the robbers

Jesus, hearing one of the robbers crucified with Him attesting to His being the Christ, turned to the man and said, "This day you will be with me in Paradise."

60 His last words before Resurrection

Jesus, at about the ninth hour, cried out and said, "*Eloi, Eloi, lama sabachthani?* My God, my God, why have You forsaken me?"

Jesus, then breathing His last, said, "It is finished. Father, into Your hands I commit my spirit."

BOOK V

The Words of Post-Resurrection Encounters

1   The first words

Jesus, as Mary Magdalene stood outside His tomb weeping, came to her and said, "Woman, why are you weeping? Whom are you seeking?"

Jesus, when Mary supposed Him to be the groundskeeper and told Him of her crucified Lord, simply said, "Mary!"

Jesus, when she recognized and cried out to Him, said, "Do not touch me, for I have not yet ascended to my Father. But go instead to my brethren and say to them, 'I ascend unto my Father and your Father, to my God and your God.'"

Jesus, when Mary Magdalene, with Mary the mother of James, was hastening to tell the other disciples about His empty tomb and the angel's message that He had risen, made Himself apparent to both of them on the path and said, "All Hail! Rejoice!"

Jesus, when they fell on the ground to worship Him, said, "Do not be afraid; but go and tell my brethren to go to Galilee and there they will see me."

2   His revealing of Himself as Messiah on the Emmaus road

Jesus, on the road from Jerusalem to Emmaus, drew near to two who had followed Him before His crucifixion and were leaving the Holy City in sorrow on the third day after His burial. He feigned being a fellow traveler and said, "What kind of conversation is this that you are having as you walk along and are so sad?"

Jesus, when they answered that He must surely be the only man in Jerusalem who had not heard of the things that had happened there, said, "What things?"

Jesus, when they told Him that Jesus of Nazareth, a mighty prophet, had been crucified and that now some of the women who had followed Him were claiming to have seen Him resurrected and among them again, said, "Oh, foolish ones and slow of heart to believe all that the prophets have said! Was it not necessary that the Messiah should suffer these things and then enter into his glory?"

3   The infusion of the Spirit in His empowering of those gathered with Him

Jesus, while His disciples and their companions were discussing earnestly what resurrection might be or mean, came among them and said, "Peace be with you."

Jesus, when they were frightened as if by seeing a ghost, said, "Why are you afraid, and why do doubts spring up in your hearts? Look here at my hands and my feet; see that it is I, myself. Touch me and see; for a ghost does not have flesh and bones as you see that I have."

Jesus then said, "Have you anything here to eat?"

Jesus, after He had eaten the broiled fish they gave Him, said, "These are my words that I spoke to you while I was still with you—that everything written about me in the Law of Moses, the Prophets, and the Psalms must be fulfilled. Thus it is written that the Messiah is to suffer and to rise from the dead on the third day, and that repentance and forgiveness of sins is to be proclaimed in his name to all nations, beginning from Jerusalem. You are witnesses of these things. And even as my Father has sent me, so I am sending you."

Jesus then breathed on them and said, "Receive the Holy Spirit. Whose sins you forgive will be forgiven them; and whose sins you do not forgive will not be forgiven. And see, I am sending upon you what my Father promised; so stay here in the city until you have been clothed with power from on high."

4   The conversation with Thomas

Jesus, on the eighth day, came among them and said, "Peace be with you."

Jesus then, seeing Thomas, the Doubter, there among them, said, "Reach here your fingers and feel my hands, and reach out your hand and thrust it into my side; and be not faithless, but believing."

Jesus, when Thomas began to reverence Him, said, "Thomas, because you have seen me, you have believed. Blessed are those who, not having ever seen me, nonetheless believe."

5   The prophecy to Peter of his martyrdom

Jesus, after the disciples had been fishing all night in the sea of Tiberias, appeared on the shore and calling out to them on their boat, and said, "My children, have you anything to eat?"

Jesus, when they told Him no, said, "Throw your net out on the right side of the boat, and you will find fish."

Jesus, as soon as they had caught a great draught of fish and brought it ashore, said, "Bring the fish you have just caught."

Jesus, who had built a fire and brought bread, took the fish and said, "Come, eat."

Jesus, after they had eaten, turned to Peter and said, "Simon, son of Jonas, do you love me more than these?"

Jesus, when Peter said he loved Him more than others, said, "Feed my sheep."

Jesus, a second and third time, addressed Peter and said, "Simon, son of Jonas, do you love me?"

Jesus, when Peter the third time asserted his love for Him, said, "Feed my sheep, for verily I tell you that when you were young, you put on your clothes and walked wherever you wished; but when you are old, you will stretch out your hands and someone else will bind you and carry you where you do not wish to go.

"Follow me."

Jesus, when Peter asked what John would do, said, "If I desire that he tarry until I come, what business is that of yours. You, follow me!"

6   The words of Ascension

Jesus, when the disciples had come to the mountain in Galilee appointed by Him as their gathering place, came to them and said, "All authority in heaven and on earth has been given to me. You have heard from me that John baptized with water, but that you shall be baptized with the Holy Spirit not many days from now. Go then and make disciples of all nations, baptizing them in the name of the Father and of the Son and of the Holy Spirit, and teaching them to obey everything that I have commanded you.

"Preach the good news to every creature; for those who believe and are baptized will be saved, but those who do not believe will be condemned. And these signs will accompany those who believe: by using my name they will cast out demons; they will speak in new tongues; they will pick up snakes in their hands, and if they drink any deadly thing, it will not hurt them; they will lay their hands on the sick, and they will recover.

"It is not for you to know the times or the seasons that the Father has in His own authority; but you will receive power after the Holy Spirit has come upon you; and you will be witnesses to me in Jerusalem, and in all Judea and in Samaria, and to the very ends of the earth. And remember, I am with you always, to the end of the age."

INDEX TO CANONICAL SOURCES

Book I. The Words of Public Teaching

1 Matthew 4:17; Mark 1:15

2 Matthew 13:57; Mark 6:4; Luke 4:18–19, 21, 23–27

3 John 5:19–47, 8:18b–19, 12:44–45, 47–50

4 Matthew 5:3–12; Luke 6:20–27

5 Matthew 5:13–16; Mark 4:21–23, 7:16, 9:49–50; Luke 8:16–17, 11:33, 14:34–35

6 Matthew 5:17–20; Luke 16:17

7 Matthew 5:21–24

8 Matthew 5:25–30, 33–42; Mark 9:43–48; Luke 6:29–30, 12:57–59

9 Matthew 5:43–48; Luke 6:27–28, 32–36

10 Matthew 6:1–18; Luke 11:2–4

11 Matthew 6:22–23; Luke 11:34–36

12 Matthew 6:19–21, 24; Luke 12:33–34, 16:13

13 Luke 12: 16–21

14 Matthew 6:25–34; Luke 12:22–32

15 Matthew 7:1–5; Mark 4:24; Luke 6:37–38, 41–42

16 Matthew 7:6

Book II. The Words of Private Instruction

1 John 3:3, 5–8, 10–21, 12:46

2 John 4:7, 10, 13–14, 16–18, 21–24, 26, 7:37–38

3 Luke 12:14–15

4 Matthew 8:20, 22; Luke 9:58–60, 62

5 Matthew 9:9, 12–14; Mark 2:14, 17; Luke 5:27, 31–32

6 Matthew 9:15–17; Mark 2:19–22; Luke 5:34–39

7 Matthew 10:5–15; Mark 6:10–11; Luke 9:3–5, 10:4

8 Matthew 9:37–38, 10:16 11:21–24; Luke 10:2–3, 5–16

9 Matthew 11:25–27, 13:16–17; Luke 10:18b–24

10 Matthew 10:17–33; Mark 8:38; Luke 6:39–40, 8:17, 9:26, 12:2–9

11 Matthew 10:37–39, 16:24–25; Mark 8:34–35; Luke 9:23–24, 12:9, 14:26–27, 17:33; John 12:25

12 Matthew 10:40–42; John 13:20

13 Luke 7:40–48, 50

14 Matthew 12:3–8; Mark 2:25–28; Luke 6:3–5

15 Matthew 13:11–15; Mark 4:11–12; Luke 8:10

16 Matthew 13:18–23; Mark 4:13–20; Luke 8:11–15

17 Matthew 13:24–33; Mark 4:26–32; Luke 13:18–21

18 Matthew 13:37–43

19 Matthew 13:44–52

20 John 6:61–65, 67, 70

21 Matthew 15:13–14

22 Matthew 15:16–20; Mark 7:14–15, 18–23

23 Matthew 16:6, 8–11; Mark 8:15, 17–21; Luke 12:1

24 Matthew 16:26–28; Mark 8:36–38, 9:1; Luke 9: 25–27

25 Luke 16:1–12

26 Matthew 17:11–12; Mark 9:12–13

27 Matthew 17:20–21; Mark 9:29; Luke 17:6

28 John 8:31–32, 34–47

29 Matthew 18:6–9; Mark 9:42; Luke 17:1–2

30 Matthew 18:10–11

31 Matthew 18:15–20; Luke 17:3

32 Matthew 18:22–35; Luke 17:4

33 Matthew 24:42–51;Luke 12:35–40, 42–48

34 Matthew 10:34–36; Luke 12:49–53

35 John 10:25–30

36 Luke 14:8–14

37 Matthew 22:2–14; Luke 14:16–24

38 Luke 17:7–10

39 Matthew 24:23–28, 37–41; Mark 13:19–23; Luke 17:22–37

40 Luke 18:2–8

41 Matthew 19:17–19, 21, 23–24, 26, 28–29; Mark 10:18–19, 21, 23–25, 27, 29–30; Luke 18:19–20, 22, 24–25, 27, 29–30, 22:28–30

42 Matthew 20:1–16

43 Matthew 20:25–28; Mark 9:35, 10:42–45; Luke 22:25–27

44 Matthew 25:14–30; Mark 13:33–37; Luke 19:12–27

45 Mark 12:43–44; Luke 21:3–4

21 Mark 9:39–41; Luke 9:50

22 Luke 9:55–56

23 John 7:6–8

24 Luke 10:41–42

25 Luke 13:32–33

26 John 11:4, 7, 9–11, 14–15, 23, 25–26, 34, 39–44, 14:29

27 Matthew 18:3, 19:14; Mark 10:14–15; Luke 18:16–17

28 Matthew 20:18–19; Mark 10:33–34; Luke 18:31–34

29 Matthew 20:21–23; Mark 10:36, 38–40

30 Luke 19:5, 9–10

31 Matthew 21:2–3; Mark 11:2–3; Luke 19:30–31

32 Luke 19:40

33 Luke 19:42–44

34 John 12:23–24, 26–28, 30–32, 35–36

35 Matthew 21:19, 21–22; Mark 11:14, 22–24

36 Matthew 24:2; Mark 13:2; Luke 21:6

37 Matthew 26:2

38 Matthew 26:10–13; Mark 14:6–9; John 12:7–8

39 Matthew 26:18; Mark 14:13–15; Luke 22:8, 10–12

40 John 13:7–8, 10–17

41 John 16:1–28, 31–33

42 Matthew 26:21, 23–25; Mark 14:18, 20–21; John 13:18–19, 26–27

43 Matthew 26:26–29; Mark 14:22–25; Luke 22:15–20

44 Luke 22:35–38

45 John 13:31–35, 15:12–25

Book V. The Words of Post-Resurrection Encounters

ACKNOWLEDGMENTS

Dozens of people have attempted to merge the varying pieces and parts of the Bible into a single, cohesive narrative. Among other things, what that means is that not a single problem I have wrestled with here is original or without precedent, save in the adoption of the Sayings format for the received text and in the categorization of the Sayings by typology. As a result, while I may have made significant decisions, I did not make them *ex cathedra* or in isolation. In the matter of ordering in particular, I am much in debt to scholars such as Burton H. Throckmorton Jr., whose work not only informs all of us who study the Scriptures, but also enables projects like this one.

Under any set of circumstances, however, whenever one is merging extant texts into an integrated whole, one is dealing with a multiplicity of factors. In *The Words of Jesus*, the merging texts involved not only the cited sections of the texts but also many variants of translation for each and every citation. My own command of Greek, which never was anywhere near athletic in the first place, has now settled into being downright arthritic, requiring crutches at every turn. There was, however, enough life left in those old linguistic bones to help carry me through. Likewise, a lifetime of fondness for and familiarity with the old *King James Version*, as well as with the new variations on it, provided me with a sense of security. In addition, I pondered with both gratitude and benefit the nuances and subtleties of what more recent scholars have done in rendering up *The Jerusalem Bible*, a long-time and much treasured friend in my private devotion; the *Revised Standard Version* and the *New Revised Standard Version*, which have informed my corporate worship experience as an Episcopalian for many, many years now; and the gifts of less celebrated translations such as the *Open Bible* and the generous aesthetic and deeply appealing accessibility of paratranslations such as *The Cotton-Patch Gospel* or Eugene Peterson's monumental *The Message*.

To say, then, that either this ordering or this translation is mine would be a lie of the worst kind. To attribute either to someone else would, however, be equally false as well as perhaps defamatory. In the end, what is rendered here is the well-mixed work of many minds and many hands, all of us in love with the same subject. My great hope is that those on whose prior work this one is built will find, if not reason to rejoice in it, then at least nothing to condemn.

Phyllis Tickle

THE AUTHOR

Phyllis Tickle is an authority on religion in America and a much sought after lecturer on the subject. She pioneered the coverage of religion publishing for *Publishers Weekly*, the international journal of the book industry. She is frequently quoted in the media (in *USA Today*, *Christian Science Monitor*, and the *New York Times*, and on PBS, NPR, and the Hallmark Channel).

In addition to presenting lectures and authoring numerous essays, articles, and interviews, Tickle is author of some two dozen books, including the widely acclaimed Stories from the Farm in Lucy trilogy released in 2004 by Loyola Press (*What the Land Already Knows*, *Wisdom in the Waiting*, and *The Graces We Remember*). Tickle is also the author/editor for the multivolume *The Divine Hours*, a series of contemporary manuals of fixed-hour prayer released by Doubleday. Tickle's most current works are *The Pocket Edition of The Divine Hours* and *The Night Offices*, both from Oxford University Press, *This Is What I Pray Today* from Dutton for Young Readers, *Prayer Is a Place* (Doubleday, 2005), and *Greed* (Oxford University Press, 2004). Other recent works include *The Shaping of a Life* (Doubleday, 2001); *God-Talk in America* (Crossroad, 1997), a spring 1998 alternate selection of Book of the Month Club's One Spirit Book Club and main selection of the Catholic Book Club; and *Rediscovering the Sacred* (Crossroad), which won a 1996 Catholic Press Association Book Award in spirituality.

Tickle began her career as a college teacher and for almost ten years served as academic dean to the Memphis College of Art, before entering full-time into writing and publishing. In September 1996 she received the Mays Award, one of the book industry's most prestigious awards for lifetime achievement in writing and publishing, specifically in recognition of her work in gaining mainstream media coverage of religion publishing. In 2004 she received the honorary degree of Doctor of Humane Letters from the Berkeley School of Divinity at Yale University, also in recognition of her work.

Tickle is a member of the Episcopal Church and has served as a Lay Eucharistic Minister and lay reader as well as, from time to time, a vestry member and teacher. She serves presently, as she has in the past, on a number of advisory and corporate boards. She is the mother of seven children and, with her physician-husband, makes her home on a small farm in rural West Tennessee.

NOTES AND REFLECTIONS

NOTES AND REFLECTIONS

NOTES AND REFLECTIONS